BUSINESS CONFIDENTIAL

BUSINESS CONFIDENTIAL
Lessons for Corporate Success from Inside the CIA

PETER EARNEST
Former Senior CIA National Clandestine Service Officer
Executive Director of the International Spy Museum

and

MARYANN KARINCH

AMACOM
AMERICAN MANAGEMENT ASSOCIATION
New York • Atlanta • Brussels • Chicago • Mexico City
San Francisco • Shanghai • Tokyo • Toronto • Washington, D.C.

Bulk discounts available. For details visit:
www.amacombooks.org/go/specialsales
Or contact special sales:
Phone: 800-250-5308
E-mail: specialsls@amanet.org
View all the AMACOM titles at: www.amacombooks.org

This publication is designed to provide accurate and authoritative information in regard to the subject matter covered. It is sold with the understanding that the publisher is not engaged in rendering legal, accounting, or other professional service. If legal advice or other expert assistance is required, the services of a competent professional person should be sought.

Library of Congress Cataloging-in-Publication Data

Earnest, Peter.
    Business confidential : lessons for corporate success from inside the CIA / Peter Earnest and Maryann Karinch.
        p. cm.
    Includes bibliographical references and index.
    ISBN-13: 978-0-8144-1448-4
    ISBN-10: 0-8144-1448-6
1. Business intelligence. 2. Success in business. 3. Organizational change. 4. United States. Central Intelligence Agency. I. Karinch, Maryann. II. Title.
    HD38.7.E27 2011
    658—dc22   2010025030

About AMA

American Management Association (www.amanet.org) is a world leader in talent development, advancing the skills of individuals to drive business success. Our mission is to support the goals of individuals and organizations through a complete range of products and services, including classroom and virtual seminars, webcasts, webinars, podcasts, conferences, corporate and government solutions, business books, and research. AMA's approach to improving performance combines experiential learning—learning through doing—with opportunities for ongoing professional growth at every step of one's career journey.

Printing number
10 9 8 7 6 5 4 3 2 1

We dedicate this book to those remarkable and courageous men and women of the Central Intelligence Agency who work long hours, make personal sacrifices, and risk their lives in the service of our country with little expectation of public acclaim.

CONTENTS

· · · · · · · · · · · · · · · · · · · ·

FOREWORD

Peter Earnest, whose distinguished career spans many years as a senior officer in the Clandestine Service, and more recently as the executive director of a highly successful business organization, has produced a work of great potential value to leaders and managers in all walks of life. Out of his own rich experience and his study of the successes and failures of others, he has identified and utilized a vast range of best practices and lessons learned that should be invaluable to all whose roles include leading and managing others, individually and as teams, in important work and service. His book could not be more timely.

In talking with people around the country, I hear their concerns over the growing threats to our national security from political and religious extremists, drug cartels, organized crime, and the thousands of cyber attacks directed against the government and private-sector corporations every day. More and more, however, I find that they wonder about our government institutions and whether they are up to dealing with today's national security threats and other challenges our nation faces.

Many of the threats they mention, of course, emerged as the Cold War ended and we entered a new millennium. It was during those years that I was privileged to serve as the director of two of our country's premier institutions dedicated to countering many such threats to our national security, the FBI and the CIA. These organizations are staffed by some of the most capable and dedicated professionals in the federal government. Having the unique opportunity to head both these organizations, I was deeply impressed with their professionalism, deep work ethic, and dedication to the country. I also saw ways that I could contribute from a leadership position.

Every director, of course, whether of the FBI, the CIA, or any other organization, inherits a new situation the day he assumes office and must take the time to gain perspective on the organization and decide how best to contribute to its effectiveness and success. During my stewardship of the Agency, I saw the need to reinforce its already tight screening process for new hires, improve mentoring/training, and enhance the assignment/promotion systems, as well as revitalize succession planning at all levels and build a relationship of trust with the U.S. Congress and those senators and congressmen who dealt regularly with the Intelligence Community.

My focus on these issues was based on my realization that we would need to build a leaner and even more efficient workforce in the future, and that the hiring and retention of valuable employees would emerge as a critical need in the coming years. This certainly proved the case as the Agency found itself in a period of shifting missions and greatly reduced resources in the lead-up to the devastating attacks of September 11th.

I agreed to provide a foreword for this book, as the authors describe so many of the positive aspects of the Agency as an organization, even noting the effects of some of my own initiatives. At the CIA, I came to know Peter from his close work with Agency leadership in his role as director of media relations and spokesman. He showed a solid grasp of the Agency's workings and an understanding of the reasons for its great successes and its highly publicized failures. His personal integrity, combined with a deep understanding of how employees can be best motivated, developed, and above all retained, makes this presentation extremely credible. So I am particularly glad to see that, in doing this book and in drawing on his wide Agency experiences, he chose to share his insights into some of the major factors that make up the CIA's organizational strengths.

Because the public is not privy to so much of the work of the CIA and of the FBI—work vital to our national security—I believe it is important for books like this one to be published. They help to counter the deliberate distortions and criticisms so often directed at the Intelligence Community, and these two organizations in particular, that we find in so many books, movies, and television.

The book's great value is in highlighting some of the best practices of the Agency, many of which you may find appropriate for your own organization. His discussion of "cracking the stovepipe" is one good example. No organization is ever perfect, but the continuing commitment of our nation's leaders to rigorous oversight and direction of organizations such as the FBI and CIA is critical to their continued vitality and success, and is a continual assurance of their being up to the task of protecting our national security.

JUDGE WILLIAM H. WEBSTER

ACKNOWLEDGMENTS

We want to express our gratitude to Judge William H. Webster for the foreword as well as to the knowledgeable and articulate contributors to this book: Jim McCormick, Gregory Hartley, Kevin Sheridan, Deborah Singer Dobson, Dean Hohl, John Naples, and a former senior operations officer who provided unique insights into the hiring process. Thanks also to Bill Sanchez and Ira Neimark; to the folks at The Charles Machine Works (aka The Ditch Witch Company) for providing some great stories; and to author/experts Ron Kessler, Tony Mendez, Keith Melton, and Daniel Pink for insights that fit well into this book. We also appreciate the enthusiastic support of our AMACOM team: Stan Wakefield, Ellen Kadin, Barry Richardson, Erika Spelman, William Helms, and Irene Majuk.

Peter Earnest—This is to acknowledge those special Agency colleagues who by their mentoring and example were models of dedicated service setting out a course that lasted throughout my career. And special thanks to my wife Karen for her staunch support and patience with the many phone calls, lengthy drafting sessions, and interminable drafts that finally culminated in this book.

Maryann Karinch—I want to thank my family and friends for the never-ending support, and my coauthor, Peter Earnest, for being an entertaining and skillful collaborator. You made me wonder, "Are all spies so charming, intelligent, and witty?" Another set of personal thanks to Michael Dobson and Ted Leemann who helped a great deal with the brainstorming process, and to the staff of the International Spy Museum for making me feel extremely welcome whenever I walk through the front door.

BUSINESS CONFIDENTIAL

How Much Is Business?
How Much Is Espionage?

by Maryann Karinch

I began this book as a skeptic, unsure that spies could teach business professionals a darned thing that was legal. After a few days of absorbing the stories and other material, I was sure they could, however. One key to seeing the connection was to ask questions that related to the actual jobs and not to the Hollywood versions of spy work. The other key was my keeping in mind that Peter Earnest is no ordinary spy. The breadth of his career experiences and his ability to communicate the lessons derived from those experiences make him a superior resource.

The result is a book offering transferable business practices from the CIA's National Clandestine Service (NCS) that support employee selection and retention, creative and agile problem solving, mission-focused outcomes, and learning from mistakes. Peter's experiences in the world of espionage illustrate core business principles. Peter and I also knew of many events from the business world that either implemented or failed to implement those principles. Including case studies from both worlds is one way this book capitalizes on his expertise and mine.

My initial vision of what this book would be was wrong in certain respects and yet, ultimately, right overall. This seeming paradox evolved as my preconceived notions about the intelligence services matured during conversations with Peter. For example, I expected a great deal of regularity: models for action with prescribed shapes and clean edges. Knowing how case officers in the field must handle each covert meeting and action with diligence, I assumed Peter would share codification of practices, formulas to achieve certain outcomes, and patterns and systems that could be replicated to improve the effectiveness of any business professional. There are some structured programs like that in the book, but for the most part the how-to guidance takes a different form.

Instead of blueprints, the recommendations here have the tone and shape of executive coaching. They flow from Peter's insights about the true success of the intelligence services: the people "on the line," why they stay there, and the advantages and functioning of a culture of trust. This is so for a couple of reasons.

First, the people "on the line" are not just case officers who recruit foreign nationals or technology wizards who will bug the lairs of terrorists abroad. They are everyone in the National Clandestine Service.

Second, the insights on why they stay at the Agency are prescient, as well as reflective of what has worked in the field for decades. In today's business world, "climbing the corporate ladder" is becoming a quaint phrase. Many people enter the workforce today viewing career advancement as a route to a purpose-driven career or simply "doing what I want to do." The Central Intelligence Agency has known since its inception that it could not lure high-caliber talent with competitive salaries alone. Intelligence officers are government employees with established pay grades. Leisure time and an evening meal with the family may often be hard to come by for case officers, who in many cases do two jobs: the cover job and the covert one.

Third, from hiring processes to communications practices through problem solving in the field, building trust both internally and externally is vital—and doing so is a calculated and achievable action. Loyalty and creative thinking are not random benefits of having good people on board. Companies can foster these attributes in a series of steps.

Having tackled business issues for thirty years as an employee, an entrepreneur, and now a writer, I especially enjoyed this project because I came to understand what kind of relationships, culture, programs, and leadership make it possible for a government agency with high demands to attract and retain so many extraordinary professionals.

Most of the answers to how-to questions came from Peter, but other sources in both the public and private sectors contributed important details as well. Using Peter's description of the Agency's successes in the key areas of personnel, operations, strategy, and learning from mistakes, I sometimes reverse-engineered the outcomes. That is, I looked for those areas of success in private companies and found out how they achieved the same results. In addition to getting glimpses of how the Agency conducts its business, therefore, I saw how companies screen employees effectively, channel the talents of their workforce to outsmart the competition, breathe life into a corporate culture, and maintain healthy management practices.

For instance, sometimes the methods used by the National Clandestine Service and by business are similar, if not identical; sometimes they look quite different. But even though NCS officers—I'll call them spies for convenience, even though the term really applies to the "other guys"—and business executives may not live similar lives, the methods they use to get their jobs done are rarely worlds apart. So organizations in the for-profit and not-for-profit sectors can implement every bit of business guidance in this book.

As for my paradox, I was wrong about what shape the how-to business information from a spy-turned-businessman would take, but I was right that it would showcase the unique insights of a successful businessman who used to be a spy. That unusual man, Peter Earnest, serves as narrator in this text—he is the "I" and "we" on the pages that reference people in the Intelligence Community. For the most part, the stories and counsel here reflect our combined experience and research—but all those stories about silent drills and dead drops . . . I had nothing to do with them.

People with Purpose:
The Heart of Success

Dedicated people are at the heart of the Intelligence Community. The CIA looks for top-notch candidates who want a mission, not just a job. This section deals with finding, recruiting, screening, and hiring the right people to fulfill that mission. They must be well trained up front and continually trained throughout their careers. They must be committed to the intelligence service, and driven to perform at a high level in a wide variety of circumstances. All of this clearly has applications in the business world as well.

· ·

CHAPTER ONE

Where Intelligence Operations and Business Meet

We handed President John F. Kennedy a slim blue folder. It contained the latest intelligence from our top source in Moscow, Soviet military intelligence Colonel Oleg Penkovsky, the weapons and military affairs expert who volunteered to provide his country's most carefully guarded secrets to the West. Passing the top-secret material to us covertly, using a dead drop under terrible time pressure, he revealed the startling limitations of Soviet missile capabilities. Now, the young president realized that the Soviets could not launch an effective attack on the United States, thus giving President Kennedy the upper hand in facing down Nikita Khrushchev during the Cuban Missile Crisis of 1962.

The mission of the U.S. intelligence services is to make sure intelligence reports going to the president and other policymakers are accurate, timely, and objective. Roughly 200,000 people, with an $80 billion-plus budget, devote themselves primarily to the production of those words. They provide information to enable decision makers to make informed choices. Recruiting agents, developing satellites, and breaking codes are among the myriad "collection activities" aimed at getting, distilling, and delivering intelligence reports.

No matter how many changes our country has experienced in deciding who is an ally and who is an adversary, the role of intelligence gathering has not changed; America's interests are paramount. And monitoring and helping to protect those interests has been our constant mission for more than sixty years. In the course of fulfilling that mission, we have brought talent, creativity, and even genius to bear in shaping and refining the business of intelligence.

Intelligence is a high-risk endeavor—a lot can go wrong. The fact that we have achieved so many successes over the years, even in the face of spectacular failures, attests to the commitment and persistence of the extraordinary men and women who have developed the field-tested practices and techniques that have brought about intelligence breakthroughs.

There have been intelligence operations throughout history, but the American services are in many ways the most highly developed intelligence-gathering organizations in the world. And the country's leadership expects much from our individual intelligence officers in carrying out the challenging requirements assigned to them to serve the country's intelligence needs.

In deciding whether or not to write this book, I asked myself, "What can businesses learn from the intelligence discipline, particularly the methods and practices of clandestine operations?" As a former Agency officer and an executive with experience as a successful independent entrepreneur, and now as a senior executive in a profitable business, I saw that the answer was: "A great deal." My reflections and observations are not meant to be prescriptive in the sense of, "This is how the Agency did it, so you should do it that way, too." Rather, they are more along the lines of, "This is what we in the Agency did and how we did it, so take these as tools and techniques that might help you accomplish your own objectives."

THE INTERSECTION OF INTERESTS

The mechanics of espionage may involve disguises, break-ins, and bugs, but the discipline of espionage is primarily about information: acquiring it, processing it, analyzing it, and providing it in clear, understandable language to decision makers. Movies focus on the mechanics because showing people talking and writing reports isn't nearly as interesting to watch. The information coming out of the field is never perfect, complete, or totally predictive. If it were, then we would be talking about facts and not the discipline of intelligence, which seeks to clarify reality to the extent possible without 100 percent assurance. Intelligence officers have to keep up with the latest requirements of their profession, the best operational practices, and breaking current affairs. They have to be prepared to respond quickly in a crisis, engage in contingency planning, and function under time pressure.

Sound like business executives?

Business executives must observe the competition at trade shows. At crowded restaurants, they must show discretion in conversation. Some are sneaky: They eavesdrop, or learn to read upside down in an attempt to pick up tidbits about a competitor. They also have to know their technology: Anything that collects, transmits, and analyzes data can be valuable to the operation.

Sound like clandestine officers?

They are obviously very much like each other in fundamental ways. If you created a Venn diagram of the primary planning and operational concerns of spies and business executives, it might look like what's shown in Figure 1-1.

The sections of this book cover these topics of common interest, drawing on my careers in both intelligence and business to highlight the lessons. Specifically, my career in the Central Intelligence Agency (CIA) began when I was recruited by the Agency during the Cold War to serve in the Agency's Clandestine Service, and then designated the Directorate of Plans and later the Directorate of Operations. I was to spend more than twenty-five years in clandestine operations in Europe and the Middle East, always under one form of cover or another.

Figure 1-1 The intersection of business and CIA interests.

People who operate well
independently and as part of a team

Product that distinguishes the company
due to its quality

**Intelligence
Operation**

Strategy leading to unique advantages

Business

Tactics that reflect street smarts
and book smarts

Outcomes meaning "We win."

Later, I would serve in a variety of positions in the Office of the Director of Central Intelligence, the so-called seventh-floor assignments representing the director and the Agency. These included an assignment heading our liaison staff to the U.S. Senate and the Senate oversight committees, another with the Agency's Inspector General overseeing the Agency itself, and finally, as the director of media relations and spokesman for the Agency under three directors: William H. Webster, the only director to head both the FBI and CIA; Robert Gates, later serving as secretary of defense under both George W. Bush and Barack Obama; and James Woolsey. These diverse assignments at Agency Headquarters and in the field enabled me to see the organization from many different perspectives throughout some of the most exciting and challenging years of the Cold War.

You can apply many of the practices I learned during my career, particularly in the National Clandestine Service (NCS),* to your own operations, whether you are a leader in your company or in a university, govern-

---

*During my years of service, it was known simply as the Clandestine Service; the word National was added in 2005, during the post-9/11 period, in which many changes took place in the structure of U.S. intelligence services.

ment office, law firm, hospital, or church. This is just as I do now, at the International Spy Museum—the first and only public museum in the United States solely dedicated to espionage.

Lots of books use games as metaphors for workplace dynamics—games such as chess, football, and rats chasing moving cheese. You leap back and forth between the two environments as you learn and apply the lessons of the game to your own situation. That approach is not what I have in mind here. Aside from occasional references to the tradecraft of espionage, the stories in this account are aimed at providing you with examples and models from my experience that you may be able to apply to your business life—how to vet, train, organize, plan for contingencies, implement plans, cut losses, take calculated risks, and increase the win ratio. And like business, espionage is more than a game.

Senior analyst Sherman Kent, one of the Central Intelligence Agency's founding fathers, saw the Agency emerge in the wake of the defunct Office of Strategic Services (OSS) and develop "recognized methodology" and "elaborate and refined techniques." He saw it become similar to other, more mature organizations, but with its own culture, élan, and sense of professionalism. In 1955, he summarized the progress as follows:

> Intelligence has become, in our own recent memory, an exacting,
> highly skilled profession, and an honorable one. Before you can enter
> this profession, you must prove yourself possessed of native talent, and
> you must bring to it some fairly rigorous retraining. Our profession like
> older ones has its own rigid entrance requirements and, like others,
> offers areas of general competence and areas of very intense specialization.
> (Kent, 1955, p.1)

Despite the steady progress the Agency has made in the fifty-plus years since Kent's statement, it is still not a perfect organization—nor will it ever be—but it does have tremendous strengths. It has attracted an extraordinary caliber of people who have not only served the goals of America but have also helped transform the Agency so that it can serve America better. They have done this through creative problem solving and bold initiatives that are consistent with our nation's values and goals. As you read on, you will see many examples of how highly the Agency values the perspective of the person doing the mission-critical job. Some of the lessons in this book, therefore, are lessons that came from the creative performances and innovative thinking of those top performers in the field—National Clandestine Service officers.

Although I give weight to success stories, I also note some of the Agency's failures that gave rise to "lessons learned," which you may find useful. What we did after botching the dismissal of operations officer Edward Lee Howard, who later sold secrets to the Soviets to get back at the Agency, contains transferable lessons. So does the policy shift we made after issuing a denial of *New York Times* reporter Stephen Engelberg's September 1985 story about defector Vitaly Yurchenko's identifying a few CIA employees as Soviet agents. Engelberg was essentially correct, and the ineffective denial made it clear that the CIA needed a better program for communicating with journalists. It's interesting to see, particularly in situations such as these, how the Agency applied lessons from well-run businesses. In the case of Howard, we set up an office to deal with employees who have problems. And in the post-Engelberg fiasco, caused by policies reflecting an adversarial relationship with the media, the Agency's new director, William Webster, departed radically from his predecessor. He brought in a public affairs officer who saw media as allies in speaking truth to power—that "power" including the American people.

DIFFERENT APPROACHES, COMMON NEEDS

Business and espionage often have dissimilar modus operandi, and the organizations that support them have some underlying differences, as well. Nevertheless, even in those areas where the two may be poles apart operationally and structurally, we can find similar needs.

First, using espionage tradecraft in business sounds sneaky, wrong, and perhaps illegal, and I don't condone using the techniques and procedures of spying to conduct industrial espionage. But for purposes of discussion in this book, I extend the concept of tradecraft to refer simply to a wide range of skills and techniques applicable to meeting challenges in business that are similar to those in the intelligence world. Think of these maneuvers as inventive ways of solving basic problems. I hope you wouldn't use a silent drill to install a bug in a rival CEO's desk drawer, but you could send a couple of staff members (not in their company polo shirts) to drop by a competitor's trade-show booth and listen to how they pitch to their prospective customers. In reading the stories of espionage in this book, you will sometimes want to focus on how we did something as much as the result we got, but in other cases I introduce more "businesslike" means of getting the same outcome.

Second, a major area of difference between espionage and business is the CIA's status as a government agency. We don't have to make money; our stakeholders—U.S. taxpayers—expect us to fulfill our mandate and to report back to the president and other senior policymakers. We are also accountable to Congress in its oversight role on behalf of the American people. Those bureaucratic advantages and constraints of congressional funding make us distinctly unlike most businesses. At the same time, you can find applicable lessons about allocation of resources and reporting practices, to name just two examples. As former Director of Central Intelligence (DCI) Richard Helms (2003) asserted with deep conviction, "The notion that secret intelligence budgets are bound only by the occasional need to break open another crate of money is pure Hollywood. Because some intelligence funds are unvouchered, there is stricter budgetary control in CIA than in any government agency I know, and throughout my tenure I remained tightfisted with the taxpayers' money."

The third major difference involves putting field officers in parts of the world that are torn by conflict, corruption, and crime. At one end of the spectrum are the inconveniences bred of pervasive corruption, right down to the cop on the corner and the guy who hooks you up to utilities. If you want to get your phone installed in a timely manner, you may have to pay someone off; it's the kind of diplomacy not taught in school. At the other end of the spectrum, you have the periodic threats to safety and security that accompany anti-Americanism. Some companies have to put employees in harm's way, too, but exposure to physical danger is not the norm. In most cases, the analogous situation has employees forced to make quick decisions to salvage a deal; the potential "harm" is financial, rather than physical. Nonetheless, both the spy and the executive need to forge critical decision-making skills and use those skills in high-pressure situations.

INSPIRATION FOR EVERYDAY EXCELLENCE

The Intelligence Community has often led the way in technological advances, so some of the devices that keep people in business connected today were once exclusive to spycraft. We developed reconnaissance satellites to spy on the Soviets, the kind of imaging that's used in tumor detection today, and the SRAC (Short-Range Agent Communications) device, which is the parent of today's cell phone. We also built scanners into pens so an agent could run it over a document and copy it; that's something you can do now, too. We have consistently placed a premium on developing and using technological advances. These technological developments are concrete examples of the many inventions, discoveries, and innovative solutions that intelligence professionals can offer you to upgrade your business practices.

With each of the sections of this book, you will step through processes and best practices that deliver competitive advantages: people who deserve to be known as operations officers, information that becomes intelligence, plans and partnerships that come together in a unified strategy, complementary tactics you can use to construct a campaign, and methods of controlling outcomes.

Keep in mind that the Intelligence Community recognizes that one officer can make an extraordinary difference in the field. So, throughout this book, you will see more focus on the performance of the individual than you do in many other business books. I don't ignore the importance of teams. I just spotlight the ways that a single person—a person with the spectrum of traits and innate abilities that make him or her extremely desirable as an employee—can help raise the competitive power of an entire organization.

To engender a shared perspective on the issues and practices of the Agency—and me as an operations officer—I thought you should see the vision and mission statements that underlie the operations of officers in the NCS, and, in fact, all intelligence officers in the Agency.

Our Vision

To be the keystone of a U.S. Intelligence Community that is pre-eminent in the world, known for both the high quality of our work and the excellence of our people.

Our Mission

We support the President, the National Security Council, and all who make and execute U.S. national security policy by:

- Providing accurate, evidence-based, comprehensive, and timely foreign intelligence related to national security; and

- Conducting counterintelligence activities, special activities, and other functions related to foreign intelligence and national security as directed by the President.

This mission statement has personal meaning for CIA officers—as every mission statement of every company should have personal meaning for its team.

The rest of this section is devoted to selecting and keeping top performers. That process begins with a clear, motivating statement that expresses what you believe with conviction about your purpose as an organization.

• •

CHAPTER TWO

What Are the Right Qualities?

Can you pick out a potential top performer from IQ scores, a Myers-Briggs profile, and hard skills? As you will see in the upcoming chapters, they can help. But I want to introduce more into the system of weighted variables that helps you create a profile of a potential top performer. This additional information includes qualities that can't be measured by the standardized tests that frightened us as teenagers, but they are real and have a bottom-line impact on the organization.

In his 2005 book *A Whole New Mind*, Daniel Pink described the characteristics and advantages of right-brained thinking. He talks about abilities that a Clandestine officer must have—and increasingly, what business executives must have to succeed. His premise summarizes why I have timely and useful information for you in this section about the kind of people you want to hire, as well as how you find and keep them:

• *L-Directed Thinking* is a form of thinking and an attitude toward life that is characteristic of the left hemisphere of the brain—sequential, literal, functional, textual, and analytic. Ascendant in the information age, exemplified by computer programmers, prized by hardheaded organizations, and emphasized in schools, this approach is directed by left-brain attributes *toward* left-brain results.

- *R-Directed Thinking* is a form of thinking and an attitude to life that is characteristic of the right hemisphere of the brain—simultaneous, metaphorical, aesthetic, contextual, and synthetic. Underemphasized in the information age, exemplified by creators and caregivers, short-changed by organizations, and neglected in schools, this approach is directed by right-brain attributes *toward* right-brain results.

Naturally, few things are solely left-brain or right-brain activities. What I want to spotlight is not an either/or but an appreciation for the interplay of the two hemispheres and to debunk any notions you might have that "smart" people are defined by test scores. Perhaps the best way to illustrate why I appreciate Pink's assessment is to describe a great CIA case officer to you.

Dick Welch struck me as very bright and quick-witted from the moment I met him. He was proud of his Irish background and the humor that came with it. Assigned to the field soon after he joined the Agency, he hit the ground running—a natural in clandestine operations because he moved easily among the circles of interest to the Agency. He seemed at ease on the political circuit, among journalists, with staffers in the embassies, and with vendors on the street. His cover could be anything that involved a lot of people. He could hold his own on the tennis court and was always a popular member of the local tennis club wherever he went. A very well-read person, he also wrote extremely well. All of that despite the fact that he had impaired vision in one eye. I mention that so that you know he was not, in fact, the perfect male specimen that Hollywood spies tend to be.

Dick formed relationships with people easily and had a knack for picking out people who had access to the levers of power in the country, and who were, therefore, good recruitment prospects. In the Clandestine Service, we recruit with the aim of enlisting someone's services as a covert source of information or to be put in a position to exert covert influence on our behalf. Sometimes, the same person serves both purposes. Since recruitment is the primary work part of the Clandestine Service's business, it's helpful to take a look at why Dick was good at it.

Dick's raw intelligence, coupled with a personable demeanor and genuine interest in people, was the foundation. He could connect through conversation and writing; he excelled at both. His contact reports were riveting. (These are memos from Clandestine officers documenting the details of an encounter with someone of interest.) The fact that his reports caught our attention meant they reflected insights and descriptive abilities that far exceeded what most people in the field had. Part of that was good training—training to recruit agents and to brief CIA superiors. But no amount of training could have made him so effective in the field unless he'd had natural abilities.

Dick was also a man of considerable personal integrity. That made him far more than a talented guy in the field: It made him someone people could trust. And recruitment does not happen without trust, except in wartime, when clear lines between friend and enemy have been drawn. Dick's colleagues, the agents he ran, his tennis buddies at the club, and his superiors at headquarters could all trust Dick.

Not everyone at headquarters necessarily saw things his way, however. I remember his telling me about some administrative assignment they directed him to do as a chief of station in a South American country. He tossed away the request and declared, "This is an Irish station!" and rejected what he saw as bureaucratic rigmarole. "Irish station" was his way of saying "my station."

Later, when Dick was assigned to Athens, he and his wife lived in the house his predecessor had lived in. The Greek Marxist terrorist group known as Revolutionary Organization November 17 knew the house. On December 23, 1975, as he and his wife were returning from a Christmas party at the ambassador's residence, the group assassinated him—not just because he was Dick Welch, a highly capable and effective CIA officer, but also because he was Dick Welch, chief of station. Killing him was symbolic, but the loss of Dick was more than symbolic to those of us left behind. We missed him as well as missed what he contributed to the CIA's success on a day-to-day basis. In 2010, the International Spy Museum opened an exhibit about Dick and his contributions to Agency successes.

Years later, I was the case officer for agents Welsh had recruited. They were still top-flight sources and they still spoke warmly and admiringly of him. You never want to lose someone that extraordinary. Never.

Dick exemplified the qualities of a top performer that Daniel Pink's book explored. Once you get someone like Dick Welch on your team, cultivate that person professionally and show your appreciation for his or her contributions. Fail to do either one and you jeopardize your success.

There are lots of people who have great ideas, but very few who know how to get things done. Business and clandestine operations have their own versions of success, but both of them need people who can get things done. Like Dick Welch.

WHO IS AN "OFFICER"?

Business uses the term "officer" to describe the top executive in a primary area, such as finance, technology, information, and security. The concept aligns closely with the military concept of an officer, with the training and acumen to make decisions on behalf of a group that reflect the vision and mission of the entire organization.

In the Agency, the cadre in the field who make up the complement of an Agency overseas post or station comprises case officers who conduct clandestine operations, communications and technical officers, people in administrative roles, and other people filling the support and administrative needs for the particular station. And just like the corporate and military meaning of the position, a case officer in the CIA's Clandestine Service is expected to be able to make decisions appropriate to both the situation and the person's rank in the organization.

The parallel with the military stops there. Although the Agency has an organizational structure that assigns rank, "just following orders" is never a good excuse for an action. A senior officer may tell junior officers to do something, but the junior officers are expected to exercise judgment and apply their unique insights. They were hired in part because they demonstrated the ability to do that.

In reviewing how the Agency defines the kind of individual who deserves to be called "case officer," you will recognize characteristics that make a good military officer or company C-level executive. I don't talk about them as applying just to people at the top of an organization chart, though. Like the Agency's Clandestine Service, you want to focus on hiring officers: people who have the right qualities so they can make a difference in your company through sound decision making and well-reasoned action. Hiring those top performers reflects the reality that a core group of individuals have the most influence in any organization. The number of those high-end contributors is disproportionate to the number of total employees, but you want to do everything possible to shrink the discrepancy.

And if you're reading this book because you aspire to be the kind of professional who distinguishes yourself by accomplishing laudable deeds for your company, here are insights based on experience to help achieve that standard of performance.

LIVE THE PARADOX— INDEPENDENT THINKING AND TEAM PLAYING

The hierarchy in espionage is not dramatically different from the hierarchy in most companies with branch offices. In the field, you're a member of the station. The head of the station is the chief of station. Typically, the station is in an official American installation. And in that facility is the "country team," headed by the lead representative of the U.S. government in the country, generally the ambassador.

The Agency wants people who can carry forward the mission under a great deal of pressure. These are people with the ability to be both strong, independent thinkers and prudent team players.

Generally speaking, it takes a couple of years for a field officer to know how to work effectively with this challenge. During a long probationary period focused on training, the individual will discover whether or not she is good at the work, and during that time, the person is preparing to do the job rather than actually doing it. It's time spent getting to know one's own reaction time, thought processes, and breadth of skills in an intimate way so that a realistic confidence can take shape. And during the course of that learning, mentoring from a senior colleague, or several of them, helps to build that self-awareness and engender loyalty to other colleagues and to the organization as a whole. The hope is that the candidate's developing skills will remain in the Intelligence service.

Living the paradox of independent thinking and team playing is critical for handling agents (the people you recruit)—and equally critical for handling customers.

When a case officer recruits, his modus operandi is similar to that of a sales professional. The primary thing being sold is himself. "They" trust the officer. The other thing an officer is selling and they are buying is the brand. In my case, it was the CIA. In the case of someone who sells iPods, it's Apple. The major difference in espionage is that the officer is establishing trust to enlist the services of an individual to act covertly—in many cases, to violate the laws of one's own country at the risk of losing a job, reputation, or possibly even one's life. That is why establishing trust in you and your institution (CIA) must be accomplished early and continuously reinforced. You often become his closest confidante, his father confessor, his best friend. But if the bond of trust is weakened, you have lost the agent.

This combination of factors is why one of the most difficult steps in handling an agent is continuity. Once you as officer recruit the agent and that person is working with you, he gets comfortable with your style. But the time will likely come that you will move on to another assignment. Turning over that agent to someone else is a skill unto itself that manifests an extraordinary ability to be a team player. In fact, you might have to be very creative in getting the agent to feel more connected to the "team" than to you personally. Sometimes the agent will balk at change because he feels his ties are to you; his trust is in you. In multiple ways throughout his relationship with you, you have to reinforce the fact that the relationship is really with the CIA, not with you as officer.

The officer who first handled Polish Colonel Ryszard Kuklinski, arguably one of the most important agents the CIA ever had, was David Forden. Even after David was transferred, he maintained contact with Kuklinski for many years by writing him letters. When he couldn't write the letters, we wrote them for him to help maintain that bond of personal trust. And the people with whom Kuklinski did have direct contact did not change often. The CIA took deliberate steps to reassure him with the same faces—combined with the continuing stream of letters from David Forden. (We made good on Kuklinski's trust. When he needed to escape the country quickly out of fear for his life, we smuggled him and the rest of his family out of Poland to safety.)

The parallel with business is unmistakable, whether the activity is sales, customer service, public relations, marketing, or any other activity that brings the people in your company in contact with the outside world for the purpose of persuading them to "trust you." It is your job to express yourself in a manner that gets them to trust "you the individual" as well as "you the representative of a team."

FOCUS ON THE MISSION

The big question that may surface for someone going through the initial screening process with the CIA may be, "Do I believe that my primary commitment is to the organization, the work, or the mission?" If the answer is "the work," then the person may end up moving on to another environment outside the intelligence services.

By contrast, if you're a lawyer hired by another government agency, having a commitment to "the work" follows the norm. You delve into the guts of your job right away and are expected to deliver top-quality product. After a couple of years, that department will have gained from your hard work and you might decide to take your experience and skills and go into the private sector, where you can make more money. You have added to the general understanding in the legal community of the operations of government, so there is a shared win. This scenario is not true in Intelligence, and for that reason, in assessing a candidate for the right qualities, interviewers and mentors go to great lengths to ascertain the level of commitment to staying with the Agency.

We have some unique challenges associated with that objective. We take upstanding young and intelligent people whose motives are high-minded, and we ask them to maintain the highest standards of integrity with their colleagues while possibly acting in violation of the laws of another country in the course of carrying out their legitimate operational assignments. We teach them how to conduct unauthorized entries, plant bugs, steal secrets, and lie—and then to return to normal when it comes time to deal with their associates at the Agency. We test people for their honesty and do background checks to ensure their patriotism; and once we see that they are exactly what we want, we help them grasp the nature and purpose of their covert work, which may involve a deviation from their ethics. We help them develop a career that serves their country while on occasion doing things that may not be legal in the country where they are assigned.

The two lessons applicable to business that come out of this situation are:

1. *The value of understanding that what you do within an organization is a role.* In other words, the job is what you do and not who you are. You can spend almost every waking moment thinking about saving people's lives if you're a doctor, but who you are is a person with the desire to save lives; how you do it is by serving as a doctor. When a case officer steals sensitive documents, he performs the service for the Agency and his country of collecting needed information. He seeks no personal gain from his actions.

2. *Allowing your mission to help motivate you to fulfill your role.* If you ever sit at your desk and wonder why you're doing whatever you're doing, consider your organizational mission statement. Hopefully, it has some value in reminding you that your goal is to "serve," "develop," or some other positive and productive activity, just as a case officer is supposed to "support the president." In the event that mission does not give you a reason to do your job, you either need a more compelling expression of it or you need a new job.

Part of the reason that there is no effort on the part of a good many professionals to adapt their work habits and point of view to a particular corporate culture is that they do not see themselves as an "IBMer" or a "GM man." They really are not tied into the mission statement. People are much more inclined to describe themselves in terms of a career: "I'm a graphic designer" or "I'm an engineer." You might work for a company, but you might also be an independent consultant, a freelancer, or a specialist who moves from company to company.

When people enter the Clandestine Service, we do not expect them to use their Agency experience as a stepping-stone to a career in another environment. Most people who apply to the Agency are aware that we recruit for the long haul, and we prefer to keep people trained in espionage within the Intelligence Community.

In saying these things about mission focus and longevity, I do not want to suggest that employees other than the "stars" lack any shred of loyalty to the company that pays them. Even though they may not see themselves as an "IBMer" or "GM man," diligent people who forgo lunches to complete a project on time or who work weekends to prepare for a meeting are giving something up for the company. Whether it's because they care about their own quality of work or they do not want a customer to be disappointed, they extend themselves. They exhibit a degree of loyalty and, on some level, an appreciation for the company mission.

In addition to the overarching mission, of course, you have the day-to-day missions—the operational exercises that reflect the main purpose of the company. If people assigned to those projects lose sight of their relevance to the big picture, when the demands of the job get intense, they might give up in a fit of "to heck with this company."

On April 6, 1978, Arkady Shevchenko made headlines worldwide. Currently serving as undersecretary-general of the United Nations, he was the highest ranking Soviet official ever to defect to the United States. In addition to my other managerial duties at Headquarters, I was assigned to head the task force handling Arkady. Until then, he was run as a covert source at the UN in New York. We were deeply concerned that Soviet Intelligence would attempt to assassinate him in the immediate aftermath of his defection. His irascible personality did not make the situation any easier. Throughout a very tense year, we kept our focus on why we were there: to debrief Shevchenko for the valuable intelligence that he provided and to ensure that President Carter would not wake up to press headlines announcing the sudden death of the most senior Soviet official to defect to America.

In 1973, Arkady had become undersecretary-general—the number-two post at the UN—and within two years, he had contacted a State Department official about defecting. That official put him in touch with the CIA.

When someone defects outright, the knowledge he has becomes dated from the moment of defection. We invariably try to convince the potential defector to stay in place. With Arkady, that attempt was successful and he remained at his post in New York until 1978, when he feared that his sudden recall to Moscow was untimely and probably a ploy to get him back to the Soviet Union and keep him there. At that point, he pleaded to defect outright.

As Shevchenko was afraid to confront his wife—he had met with resistance when he vaguely raised the issue of defection with her before—a combined team of CIA and FBI officers whisked him out of New York at night and brought him to a safe house in Virginia. We began a series of debriefings focused on Soviet policy thinking and decision making, his tasks on behalf of Soviet Intelligence (the KGB) at the UN, and other details about his relations with and impressions of Soviet leaders.

One of my principal debriefers was Aldrich "Rick" Ames, later notorious for his own eventual betrayal and highly damaging espionage on behalf of the KGB. (More on that in a later chapter.) Rick did a journeyman's job in relating to Shevchenko and helping to arrange debriefings of him by other members of the Intelligence Community. The two-man FBI team assigned to the task force was headed by a highly experienced FBI counterintelligence special agent named David Major. We worked closely together to protect Shevchenko, sometimes from himself. A temperamental man who relished his vodka, he refused to consider resettling in this country under a different name, and he also refused to give up his pursuit of call girls, a practice that had gotten him into more than one scrape in New York City.

Arkady would become incensed with my requests about the schedule of briefings, his demands, his trips; he would "fire" me on a regular basis. I was the most senior guy he had to deal with, so he couldn't "fire" me and, in the end, we had a good relationship. However, the FBI men on our team faced a new world of duties with Arkady. They had to take him shopping and protect him against being discovered when one of his invited "girls" would visit. At one point, I gave the FBI agents a considerable amount of money to take him to the Caribbean for a vacation. When I counted out the money in thousand-dollar bills, they expressed astonishment, saying they were used to strict FBI procedures regarding expenditures. They said, "Nobody can hand out money like that except God!"

So they started calling me "God" among themselves, and occasionally also around a woman named Judy Chavez whom Arkady was seeing regularly. Chavez later led him into a media ambush, resulting in much undesired media play, and she went on to author a book about her relationship with him, titled *Defector's Mistress*. In that book, she talks about the special agents, referring to a mysterious figure called "God," who figured in the background. (Regardless of how it may appear, my use of Agency funds was strictly audited at the conclusion of the task force.)

We were a closely knit team, fixed on protecting one person who represented a way to achieve our organizational mission. In some ways, our relationship with him was akin to the way a solid team responds to a difficult new CEO. You suck it up and say, "It's for the good of the company. We have to remember why we're here."

FIRST, DO NO HARM

Loyalty to country is a concept that most Americans, and most people of other nationalities, believe in and live by. Loyalty to the company that employs you—as opposed to one that you or a relative founded—doesn't necessarily carry the same weight or sense of transcendence.

Nevertheless, the company's executives, board, and shareholders have a right to expect that you won't do any harm to the company; there is an expectation of passive loyalty. In other words, go ahead and accept your paycheck and complain about your boss and colleagues at home, but do not do anything to undermine the company or publicly embarrass the people you work with. If you find yourself doing that, you should give serious thought to leaving.

The ultimate display of disloyalty is the betrayal of someone like Agency Intelligence Officer Aldrich "Rick" Ames. An employee of Microsoft who badmouths the company without offering any constructive criticism to company officers does not commit the same kind of high crime against country and neighbors as Ames did, but he doesn't deserve any more of Microsoft's money, either.

Intelligence officers tend to be a very critical bunch, just like the top performers in any company. They ask themselves, and each other, the tough questions about what went wrong and whose fault it was, or what went sort of right that could have been a bigger victory. If you put a handful of them in an office together, you might hear things like, "I can't believe that guy's an operations officer. He couldn't run an operation in his kid's playpen." That's a complaint in the presence of peers. Put the same guy at a booth in a crowded restaurant where his comments may easily be overheard, and it is highly likely he will be more discreet.

More than being critical of others, however, intelligence officers tend to be self-critical. A healthy ego allows them to talk about what went wrong and what they could have done better, without any loss of self-esteem. They focus on the mission, and on the success of operations meant to achieve it, making this kind of self-analysis and self-corrective action essential exercises.

To take advantage of that predilection for criticism, the Agency institutionalizes it. The Inspector General's Office, which is where I spent three years, puts all of its resources into answering the compound question, "What's not working—and why?" Virtually all government agencies have an audit process that may or may not be associated with something called the "inspector general," so this audit exercise is not inherently unusual. It probably is unusual the way the Agency carries it out, however, and I explore that in more detail in Section 3 of this book, "Organizational Improvement."

PUT PASSION TO WORK

When I was serving as the CIA spokesman, I was occasionally visited by a reporter from a major weekly news magazine who said, "I just love coming here. It isn't like any other government agency I visit." I thought he was referring to an aura of secrecy, or the knowledge that somewhere, just around the corner, was a spy with hot stories, but he wasn't. He said that coming to the Agency made him feel energized, even uplifted, because everyone seemed to project a genuine sense of purpose. I think his words were, "People seem crisp and purposeful. Focused on a common goal."

It's demoralizing to spend forty to fifty hours a week working for a company where you are discontent. People do it all the time for the paycheck, but I ask you to consider that passion and a sense of purpose can, and should, be your guide in a practical way. You need to pursue the professional company of people you respect. It is not good enough to pal around with a few people and share a common enemy—like the boss; just having something or someone in common to complain about does not compensate for a lack of passion and purpose. All you are, then, is a wage slave.

At the risk of sounding like I'm advocating putting Prozac in the drinking water, I'd like to emphasize that passion for the mission not only engenders loyalty and productivity among employees but also contributes to their high sense of purpose, even in the face of personal or professional difficulties.

DELIVER COMPETENCE, NOT HEROICS

One characteristic permeates the definition of "intelligence officer" more than any other: professional competence. Because it surfaces in different ways depending on the circumstance, professional competence encompasses all of the other traits described in this chapter, such as sound decision making, quick-wittedness, common sense, and critical thinking.

Depending on the type of position, competence might transfer very well from one environment to the other. William Webster had a successful tenure as head of the FBI, and a successful tenure as head of the CIA. Many generals—George Washington, among them—performed with excellence on the field of battle and equally well in the role of head of state.

Transferability also depends on the individual's ability to manage the transition from one environment to another, and to make the connection between the two. Former Director of Central Intelligence William Casey brought his friend, stockbroker Max Hugel, into the CIA as his special assistant. The two had known each other from work on the 1980 Reagan presidential campaign. Hugel wanted more responsibility, so Casey made him head of the Directorate of Operations, the most sensitive job in the CIA. Central to determining whether or not the appointment was a mistake was Hugel's ability to transfer his competence, rather than his professional background as a stockbroker. In this case, Hugel quickly found himself battling accusations of improper conduct by previous business associates, as well as discontent and disrespect from inside the Agency. He was out on the street two months later. In contrast, John McCone was arguably one of the best directors the Agency ever had, but at the time his selection seemed less than wise. He was a businessman—what could he know about being in the hot seat of the nation's Intelligence Community? But McCone had the right qualities of judgment and leadership, and he knew how to bring them to bear in his government service. McCone's knowledge of the new environment and challenges came quickly, and one could conclude that he readily saw how to leverage his expertise. Max Hugel's highly publicized failure seemed to be that he did not, or could not, do that.

I want to draw a clear distinction here between competence and heroics, because it's competence that any organization needs, though it's heroics that catch our attention and often lead to thunderous applause (or promotion). What's the basic difference? If you can call the feat an accomplishment resulting from training and good judgment, then it's competence; if you can call it a stunt, it's heroics.

James Bond does amazing things that no real case officer could do, no matter how much training he or she had; they are stunts. Captain Chesley B. "Sully" Sullenberger III, whose emergency landing of the US Airways jet in the Hudson River on January 15, 2009, prevented the loss of 155 lives, did something that regular people could do with the right training and experience, even though many might not have had his courage and presence of mind. He did his job. He is impressive because he has the ability to repeat extraordinary performance and maybe even to teach it to others, at least through demonstration.

The Agency isn't perfect, but there is a culture of appreciating competence and of not offering reinforcement to show-offs. In fact, we do more than just keep an eye on people whose ego outstrips their performance. We find a place for them outside of operations—maybe so far outside that they have to find a job elsewhere. In contrast, tireless self-promoters and stuntmen tend to do quite well in business. The worst possible examples are people like Bernard Madoff, who dazzled investors with unbelievable returns. Why didn't people see him as a comic book "hero" of finance—doing the impossible, so that it must, indeed, be impossible?

On a less dramatic scale, companies commonly sabotage their own success by rewarding the people who do backflips in the end zone after scoring a touchdown. These are people who refer to themselves as star performers, rather than wait for kudos from people who appreciate their work. When companies promote the self-promoters with hollow performances, it's a setup for the famous Peter Principle: "In a hierarchy, every employee tends to rise to his level of incompetence."

The most respected and productive case officer—someone who has the spectrum of right qualities—is a normal human being who can replicate excellent performance, who demonstrates simple competence.

WHAT ARE THE RIGHT QUALITIES?

- Mental strength—a balance of native intelligence, quick wittedness, and resilience rooted in a healthy ego

- Independent thinking that gives rise to creative problem solving

- Respect for team colleagues that acknowledges the mission they share

- Loyalty that supports constructive criticism and discourages comments and actions harmful to the team or organization

- Passion for both the mission of the organization and the work itself; it's the drive to *want* to deliver 110 percent

- Commitment to competence, not heroics

. . . .

CHAPTER THREE

Hiring to Support Your Mission

"In a democracy such as the United States, egalitarian sentiment runs strong and deep, and elitism in almost any form is suspect. For those who grew up believing that anyone could be president, it's not a big leap of logic to conclude that anyone should be able to become a case officer in the CIA."

—Former senior CIA operations officer **Duane "Dewey" Clarridge**,
  A Spy for All Seasons

The Agency historically has gotten a lot of applicants because many people find the CIA and its mission alluring. They have visions of travel, intrigue, and meeting interesting people in the most unique work environment in the world. When I was at Headquarters in the early 1990s, we were averaging 150,000 applicants a year. There were even more in the wake of the September 11, 2001, attacks. In addition to the applications from recent college graduates, military officers, and people with careers in which they don't find a sense of purpose, you also see a number of wannabes, who may consider their striking resemblance to Daniel Craig as a real qualification.

When you're an organization that has applicants who range from petty criminals to the best and brightest in the nation, you have to have a system that efficiently weeds out people with the "wrong stuff," so that the resources you allocate to training after hiring are investments with good returns.

The hiring process involves stages of screening, testing, and final interviews, with each stage advancing toward identification of the top candidates. Former operations officers and other people who are doing the job you are interviewing for are involved in the intake process from the very beginning. Once you are hired and enter a probationary period of up to three years, those and other experienced officers will continue to evaluate you continuously, day after day.

It takes substantial resources to be so thorough in hiring, so it's no surprise that companies generally don't do anything close to this level of screening, testing, and evaluation. They hire with skill proficiency in mind, and maybe give some credits for personality, depending on the job. For the practical reason of high turnover cost, it is in the Agency's (and the taxpayers') best interest to spend the time on and allocate seasoned personnel to a lengthy hiring process. What makes that course of action financially feasible, of course, is that we don't have to make a profit and we do have a budget authorized by the U.S. Congress that is commensurate with our vital mission. I hope this book makes it possible for you to come closer to the Agency's process without the R&D investment that we had to make.

If you consider the cost of failure for the Agency, putting a lot of resources into the hiring process makes perfect sense. When someone like former Agency officer Edward Lee Howard gets disgruntled about the way he's been treated, and he starts selling secrets to the enemy, people die. Howard was a junior case officer undergoing training for handling clandestine assets (i.e., sources) in Moscow. In the course of his preparation, the Agency learned that he had been using drugs and had engaged in petty theft in the past. Those actions disqualified him for the assignment, and he was summarily fired.

Bitter at his abrupt dismissal, Howard later volunteered to provide his inside knowledge to the KGB, the Soviet intelligence service. He deserved to be fired for lying about illegal drug use, but he was hired and fired badly. In the wake of his betrayal, the Agency took steps to improve the dismissal process to avoid alienating future dismissed employees. The cost of failure for some companies is generally not a life-and-death matter, but sometimes it is. Companies that make helicopters, build bridges, and write software for medical facilities can create life-threatening problems when their projects fail.

Regardless of whether or not your company engages in ventures that could even remotely be considered life-and-death projects, using the excuse of budget constraints to trim the interview process is a real mistake. Employee turnover is a significant cost of doing business. *Business & Legal Reports* (www.BLR.com) offers a calculator to determine the cost of replacing an employee. I ran the numbers reflecting my own business experience, and I found their estimate of 30 percent of annual compensation to be conservative; some executive positions would easily take that cost up to 60 percent. Their matrix covers three major areas: cost factors for the department, which focuses on compensation; cost factors for human resources, or whoever has the lead in the hiring process; and other costs in total dollars, such as placement agency fees, testing, and training. In addition, you have the cost of lost productivity, which may or may not be something you can calculate.

The turnover cost for the Agency is much higher. In fact, a rough estimate might place it at well over twenty times the salary that the employee is paid. Some of the factors that push this number up are the exit interview, the screening process for new applicants, interviews, reference checks, and something that *BLR* calls "new employee orientation." Interviews alone for the Agency might be anywhere from forty-five minutes to nearly four hours—and there are a number of them.

Even though the Agency's turnover rate has historically been low by private-sector standards—roughly 5 percent for years—neither the CIA nor any twenty-first century company should harbor illusions about job-seeking individuals in the present generation seeking to become "company men." We don't want to spend a couple of years training people, only to have them take all of the mental, emotional, and physical conditioning and move on to jobs outside of the Intelligence Community—but it happens. Service in the Intelligence Community is a strong credential, and there are people in both operations and analysis who use it as an entrée to higher-paying positions in the private sector.

Realistically, people who go into the Agency, particularly into operations, are not usually effective for two or three years; they need seasoning first. The loss of a trained officer leaving for a job outside the Agency is harder to mitigate than the loss of a junior lawyer from the Justice Department, where the department would have gotten two or three years of solid work out of him. And there's the corollary advantage for the federal department: That lawyer well trained in federal operations who goes into the private sector raises the general level of knowledge about how government works. In contrast, the Agency doesn't get that kind of return on investment. We generally get no benefit when a Clandestine officer leaves the CIA and takes what he knows to the private sector, although there are situations in which people come back and perform valuable services as contractors. And so, we have to look at a spectrum of qualifications beyond academic achievement in selecting a new officer. Sense of purpose is key.

If you want to be taken seriously so that you are tagged as someone who has the ability to make a long-term commitment, or at least will give 100 percent while you're there, then come into the interview process prepared. On the flip side, if the organization wants to be taken seriously as an employer worth your commitment, then certain practices must be in place before you even interview for a position.

PREPARING TO HIRE

An organization that regularly draws high-caliber people has characteristics and policies worth perpetuating. You will defer offers from others and even work for less money to secure a position in that company. It's a place where employees use the phrase "want to" rather than "have to."

Kevin Sheridan, founder of HR Solutions (www.hrsolutionsinc.com), has honed a concept he calls a Magnetic Culture™, a term he uses in advising client companies on their hiring practices. Although the Agency does not use this nomenclature to describe its culture or the process of creating such an environment, Kevin's concept is similar and is valid for this discussion of Agency policy.

Kevin describes an environment that draws top talent to the organization and that continuously attracts new talent, making it difficult for high performers to leave because they feel the magnetic pull—the attraction of the culture. After years of exploring the "how to" of engaging employees early and often, Kevin has learned that an organization must engage employees even before they come in for the job interview: "Engagement begins the first time they hear the company name."

In terms of brand or name recognition, the CIA has an advantage over most private companies. But name recognition alone does not establish the magnetism that makes people want to work for the Agency. In any recruiting encounter, any posting of career opportunities at the Agency, and any media outreach to potential employees, the Agency has to emphasize the value of its mission, which is the foundation for its corporate culture.

Johnny "Mike" Spann, the first combat victim in Afghanistan during the combined Agency and Special Forces efforts to drive the Taliban out of that country following al-Qaeda's 9/11 attack, was a CIA case officer. After his death on November 25, 2001, family members recalled his saying, "Someone's got to do the things that no one else wants to do." His words captured one reason the Agency's mission has such strong pull: Operations officers see their work as vital to the national security of their country.

Kevin Sheridan has noted that "as long as people believe in the mission of the organization, they remain with the organization." His strategy is to create passionate believers. During the recruiting process, he explains, it is crucial to convey the culture as one where people are passionate about the organization's mission, passionate about what they do on a day-to-day basis. Kevin says, "Believers are confident they can create wonderful outcomes contributing to the culture of magnetism and the desired outcome of the organization—that is, the mission."

Organizations fail to attract the kind of people they desperately need if the company's message, or brand, is either never promoted to prospective employees or is promoted poorly. Another cause for this failure is having a message that falls on deaf ears because the recruiting is being done in the wrong place. That is, the person doing the recruiting doesn't have the process in place to find the right people. A good recruiter starts with introspection—looking at the company and recognizing what characteristics have proven to work in that culture, so that new employees will thrive and grow and so the organization will improve as a result of their being there.

Kevin believes that opportunity and need are especially acute in the Intelligence Community. "I'm sure a lot of people are initially attracted to the career because they have fallen under the spell of James Bond movies, and they have a picture of the duties as a Hollywood adventure, rather than as the reality of day-to-day service. That leads to disenchantment if they find out their activities don't match their expectations." The reason this disenchantment doesn't happen in almost all cases is that the Agency works hard at managing expectations.

To promote that healthy "magnetic culture," and not have employees sense a bait-and-switch, honesty must prevail in the recruiting process. You have to communicate the exciting part of the job, but you must also explain the mundane and routine—albeit essential—tasks that support the organization's overall mission. You won't find anyone in the Agency promoting a Hollywood version of a spy's daily schedule: Wake up leggy Kazakhstani supermodel. Grab PPK and shoot bad man hiding under bed. Remind room service morning martini should be shaken not stirred. Beat E.V.I.L. second-in-command in fencing match. Steal his woman for lunchtime tryst. Get her to help kill E.V.I.L. leader at dinner. Return to hotel. Remind room service evening martini should be shaken not stirred. Take leggy Kazakhstani supermodel to bed.

SCREENING

In the world of security, profiling puts people into categories based on dress, appearance, mannerisms, and other external characteristics, as well as their political or religious orientation. In this environment, simply having a dark complexion and a three-day beard might cause delays in getting a boarding pass.

In the world of private industry, however, this level of profiling cannot legally involve attributes such as religion and basic physical appearance, though in an unstated way it still does. A simple behavioral habit or other observable factor about you can activate a particular response because it represents something the interviewer considers an element of a "bad" profile. One little thing can evoke an automatic rejection—the way you dress, an accent, a weird laugh. Commonly, people who prepare for job interviews are well aware of this and try to adapt for the occasion. Look at how often that backfires, though. Going to a job interview wearing makeup to hide an outrageous tattoo conveys the impression that you think the tattoo could distract from your effectiveness as a business professional. To then uncover the tattoo after hiring and expect people to ignore it might be a stretch. You were "profiled" on the basis of your interview appearance, which turns out to be a false representation.

On one hand, Agency interviewers must scrupulously avoid letting irrational subjective, and probably subliminal, judgments interfere with their evaluations. In the early days of the Agency, when alumni of Ivy League schools staffed a good deal of the organization with more of their own, they relied on a form of networking, with the best of intentions; it was a kind of profiling that became an element in seeking out qualified people. Now, the Agency's workforce reflects the general makeup of our society—New Age and traditional, conservative and liberal, male and female.

On the other hand, knowing that no interviewers can be totally objective, the Agency tries to employ profiling in a positive way. The whole purpose of having folks who have been in the field do the initial screening interviews is to bring their subjective judgment to bear, as well as gather objective data. The underlying question in the interviews is, "Could this person be one of us?"

THE INITIAL INTERVIEW

The road to becoming an NCS officer is a long one, but not necessarily longer than the equivalent in some large companies, which also conduct screening and testing over a period of months, or even for more than a year. For example, until the past couple of years, Google was notoriously secretive and lengthy in its interview process, exceeding the five to eight interviews per candidate considered typical in Silicon Valley.

With a prospective case officer, the process begins rather conventionally with an application, readily found at www.cia.gov. It progresses through interviews, and then moves into somewhat less common types of physical and psychological tests, including a polygraph, and then an intensive background investigation.

After a candidate's application gets a favorable review, the interviews begin. Each time the individual goes through an interview, she is progressing through the application process. At each level, the applicant learns a little more about the organization and what will be expected of her. By the time the person completes the application process and receives a conditional offer of employment, she will have a good grasp of what the work would involve.

The first interview is around forty-five minutes; the others may be more than three hours each and occur over several months. In the course of those interviews, the candidate learns not only about the organization and the probable duties but also what to expect in terms of support from the organization during the service as a Clandestine officer.

Someone who has done the kind of work that the candidate aspires to do conducts the initial phone interview, rather than someone from personnel. F.B., a former Directorate of Operations officer who serves that function, explains, "We talk with the applicants to get a feel for their motivation. Is this someone who sees a career in the National Clandestine Service as exciting and fun, or is he looking deeper, hoping to contribute something to national security?"

With a copy of the application in front of her, someone like F.B. calls the individual who has made it past the personnel office's basic screening. The reasons for not making it past the initial screening are fairly straightforward. The most obvious is that the person is not a U.S. citizen. Although the Agency needs people with fluency in particular languages and cultures, the person still has to be a citizen. Logical candidates might include people from military families whose mother or father brought the family along when being stationed abroad.

When F.B. sets up an appointment for the interview, she encourages the applicant to review the information on the Agency's Web site. Usually, the interview occurs within two days of that call.

As with an interview for almost any organization, the applicant talks about his reasons for making whatever changes are necessary to work for the Agency. And since the individual would be living overseas much of his career with the NCS, as well as moving every few years, it's essential that there be buy-in from the spouse.

This is one aspect of the Agency interview process that companies might learn from, but not necessarily be in a great position to adopt. Since it isn't uncommon for people in many kinds of sales and executive positions to work overtime, travel extensively, and bring their work home—even if it's just bringing it home mentally—the question of family engagement is an important one. Simply asking, "What does your spouse think about your applying for a position that requires you to travel half the time?" can give you insights into how long the applicant has wanted a job like this and how excited he is about getting an interview. But simply asking that question might also get you in trouble with HR. Ask for the guidelines on this. It is key information, but you have to get it legally.

In addition to commitment and a sense of purpose, one of the things that the Agency looks for in a successful applicant is a high tolerance for ambiguity. In a complex world that forces operational changes, it may often be hard to have a yes or no answer to a question. As a corollary, a given problem may not always have the same solution every time. Some people do not have a tolerance for those kinds of variables; they are used to a more structured organization. Being able to make decisions quickly, without someone senior to guide them, just isn't something many people can handle. It isn't as though they are unable to contribute to the organization; they just aren't cut out for work in the field.

Those who believe they can thrive in the face of such ambiguity know instinctively that the more experiences they have that require agile decision making, the better they will get at it. There is an incremental buildup in the skill set that supports that kind of thinking, making a person increasingly more valuable to the organization.

Red flags in the interview process fall into categories any experienced human resources professional would recognize. There are shallow answers: "I want to work for the organization because I love to travel." There are self-sabotaging admissions: "This job is a great opportunity to forget about my failed marriage." There are victim responses: "I've been criticized unfairly so many times." And F.B. has even heard people try to impress her with their computer skills by saying things like, "My old boss treated everyone in our department so poorly that I planted a worm on his computer that affected the files on his hard drive. But only on *his* hard drive."

Later interviews reveal information about the person's integrity, street smarts, self-esteem, interpersonal skills, intuition, and other aspects of personality and experience that indicate he deserves the title "case officer" and the responsibility that title implies. The Agency looks for people with solid egos, but not arrogance that would somehow shade what they're doing. The Agency also wants risk takers, but not thrill seekers or daredevils. They are people who, in the words of Jim McCormick (2008), author of *The Power of Risk*, know how to take "intelligent risks"—which involve evaluating options, mitigating danger, and seizing opportunity when it presents itself. They are people who can tackle extraordinary challenge with their eyes on the rewards as they relate to the Agency's mission. In short, the interviewers are looking for indications that the person has the kind of life experiences, personality, and degree of intelligence that would make him suitable for life in a covert career.

The nature of the initial interview puts a number of people at a decided disadvantage. If you do not have or cannot demonstrate smooth verbal and written communication, your great credentials might count for little and you might find yourself guided to positions outside the NCS, where there is not as high a requirement for people skills.

Signs the Candidate Really Wants the Position	Red Flags
Buy-in from spouse on special demands of job, such as travel, long hours, quirky hours	Hasn't discussed special demands with the spouse or partner
Able to articulate good reasons he finds the company a desirable place to work	Has no clue what's special about the company as it relates to his career goals or preferred work environment
Sense of curiosity, as well as optimism, about what will be expected on the job	Seeming inflexibility about doing anything other than what's in the job description

Moving Through the Interview Process

Once an applicant gets through that initial screening, she meets with someone about whom the applicant knows nothing. This is generally a different scenario from the corporate world, in which an applicant is told that the interviews will begin with the human resources manager, and the vice president of a division, and then a couple of other people, all of whom have names and titles. The applicant can do homework on those people to prepare for the meetings or even use Google Earth to find out what their neighborhoods look like. You can go on LinkedIn, Plaxo, and Facebook to find out something else about their professional contacts and colleagues.

As the United States plummeted into a recession in 2008 and 2009, and every media outlet from daily newspapers to business publications to blogs offered case studies and advice to help job seekers, certain tips surfaced over and over—and they centered on research. Specifically, the recommendations were to use Web-based resources, and pay for them if you must, to be able to say something of substance in a job interview. Know enough about the company's people, history, and problems to engage in meaningful conversation and perhaps pose a provocative question or even suggest an approach to solving a current problem.

At the Agency, the applicant is at a slight disadvantage. All that's known is that you have an interview with someone, or perhaps a few people. But preparing for those encounters involves some considerations that candidates for any position in any environment should consider; it all goes back to the value of doing your homework:

• *Know something about the organization.* You may think that's obvious, but I have been with a roomful of candidates and asked them who had read a book about the Agency. Maybe three hands go up. With a wealth of online resources, there is no excuse for walking into a job interview without a grasp of the organization's mission, history, organizational structure, products and services, external communications such as brochures and press releases, and public reputation. The CIA, for example, is a frequent target of sharp media and public criticism, and comes up in all media of popular culture, books, movies, TV, and so on. What's your view? Do you agree with some criticism? Disagree? Why? The CIA makes it easy for candidates to know some of what they could be reading because the Agency's recommended reading list is published on its Web site. These materials give specific information about what the organization is and what it is not. Whether or not the candidate even noticed the list tells the interviewer something salient.

• *Have a grasp of current affairs.* Just as an applicant to the Agency ought to have some grasp of world developments, particularly concerning the involvement of the United States or threats to national security, a job applicant at a company should have knowledge of the marketplace where the company competes. An interviewer might ask a question like "Can you briefly discuss an issue that's been in the news that you think would be of interest to the company's board of directors?"

   If someone applied for a media-relations job at the International Spy Museum, where we charge admission, and he didn't know that the museums of the Smithsonian Institution in Washington, D.C., all of which are in competition with one another to some extent, do not charge admission, then that person lacks important information.

He does not have a decent sense of what would be "current affairs" in our context—that is, our marketplace. The applicant wouldn't be expected to know precise details, such as the fact that the Smithsonian was established by an act of Congress so it receives a great deal of federal money (about 70 percent of its budget), but I would expect him to know that the International Spy Museum is a private institution—that is, don't walk in thinking you're applying for a government job.

I have a friend who applied for a job in the media-relations department of a computer group early in her career, and during the interview, she was asked what she thought she'd be writing about. She completely missed the mark on the question because the glaring, front-page issue was ergonomics, such as radiation from monitors and keyboards related to carpal tunnel syndrome, and she was focused on unrelated technological advances.

- *Leverage your connections—but carefully.* Many organizations, including the Agency, have become sensitized to favoritism in hiring because of highly publicized and embarrassing hiring blunders over the years in both government and the private sector.

- *Have a sense of purpose as it relates to the environment.* If you don't care about the organization you work for, you are at a distinct psychological disadvantage in competing against people who do care about their employers. Conducting espionage operations abroad is a public service, albeit done in secret; the American people both pay you and depend on you to do it well. You may find the career path attractive because you think there's adventure involved, but the American people want you to be fully engaged even when there is no adventure involved.

Companies also suffer when there is no connection between the organization and the employee. I have a former colleague who briefly went to work for a very large computer company because "the money was good." The company recognized that he had the right credentials for a high-paying, senior position and hired him without even trying to determine whether he appreciated the corporate mission or culture. Aside from seeing a gigantic paycheck every two weeks, he found no substantive reason to perform well. He left after a year, probably moments before they were ready to boot him out the door.

The Agency	Company XYZ
Know something about the organization	Know something about the company
Have a grasp of current affairs	Have a grasp of the market conditions in which the company operates
Leverage your connections cautiously	Leverage your connections sensibly; don't spotlight them—those connections should be paving the way for you without your throwing them around
Have a sense of purpose as it relates to the Agency; keep in mind that intelligence gathering is a public-service career	Have a reason for wanting to join this company as opposed to another one; identify who the company serves and how it serves them well
Identify your core strengths and see if they align with those the Agency needs in a case officer; don't waste your time or anyone else's trying to fake it	Identify your core strengths and see if they align with those required for your role in the company; if not, highlight your strengths and see what other positions might be available

TESTING

Test for the positives—good team player, profile of a manager, skills—but don't forget the testing for negatives as well. Some of the screening the Agency does relates to weeding out characters with negative traits. The polygraph is just one of the tests we use to do that. In industry, you don't have to screen for negatives in a criminal or moral sense, but you do it as a matter of course to protect yourself from hiring victims and losers, as well as people who are ill-suited for the position. *Business & Legal Reports* very conservatively estimates that the 2010 cost to a company of hiring a single executive is about $12,100, if you include factors such as a percentage of HR's time and hard costs of recruitment. One of the smallest amounts in their calculation is pre-employment testing—$750.

In assessing people to determine whether or not their psychological makeup matches well with the roles you have in mind for them, consider how much anxiety you save the applicants, as well as yourself, with a well-administered test. Maryann was a speech and drama major in college. Based on that, you could conclude she probably would not make a career loan officer, but she nevertheless applied for a job with Household Finance Corporation (HFC) immediately after graduation. Her thinking was, "I'll be dealing with people, which is a plus, and I can earn some good money to help pay for graduate school." Fortunately, at the very first interview HFC administered a simple test, probably something in the family of the Myers-Briggs Type Indicator or the Minnesota Multiphasic Personality Inventory. The counselor then called her into his office and humanely rejected her: "It would be fun to work with you, but not here." She breathed a sigh of relief and took his advice to find something more suited to her disposition and interests.

Dick Welch, whom I profiled in Chapter 2 as an example of a top performer in the CIA, was a Harvard-educated classicist. Based on my training with the Myers-Briggs, I speculated he and I had similar profiles: extrovert, intuitive, thinking, and perceiving. It's highly likely HFC would not have hired either one of us, either.

Testing for Leadership

Before I go into the standardized ways of testing for leadership, I want to state that I don't know any companies, including the Agency, that invest more confidence in a test than in actual performance. The ultimate leadership test is this: Will people choose to follow the applicant? And not everyone should aspire to leadership—in fact, one would hope that many highly talented people aspire to management instead.

I think of managers as having organizational skills and leaders as having inspirational skills. Inspiration without organization does not work. Leadership is about being able to motivate, engage, hire, and lead other people. It's reasonable to expect that a leader has abilities and characteristics such as integrity, follow-through, and vision. These are strategic abilities. In contrast, management is about being able to structure time and allocate resources on a day-to-day basis. It requires tactical abilities.

One of two factors is responsible for when people put into leadership positions fail: Either they might not have the personality of a leader and should not be placed in such a demanding position, or no one recognized the person's need for training. Testing can avert the failure, but don't wait to do it until someone is about to be promoted. Assessing leadership potential is different from assessing individual performance skills. Leadership acumen requires both the right personality and the right set of talents. Ideally, you want to assess this as a person joins the company, as a way of determining her potential.

Companies commonly make the mistake of assuming that someone with strong independent-worker skills will magically grow leadership skills when placed in a leadership position, or that those skills can be cultivated in the person because she is intelligent and capable. Someone who works in a hospital might be a phenomenal clinician, for example, and be widely admired in the organization. However, this innovative, technical expert may eventually be promoted to a leadership position and then unexpectedly fail.

Some in the Agency are innovative experts who are outstanding in their fields, but are not cut out for managerial, let alone executive, positions. We appreciate them for the fine employees they are, and we look for ways to recognize their contributions, perhaps in the form of raises, but we do not want to make the mistake of promoting them beyond their leadership capabilities.

The Myers-Briggs Type Indicator (MBTI) and other forms of personality and performance assessment instruments are widely used, as are 360-degree evaluations in which feedback is solicited from an employee's supervisors, peers, and subordinates. MBTI has been used in Agency training as a way for participants to assess themselves and to develop a more accurate sense of how others see them. Observing the degree to which employees quickly develop insight into their own personalities and how they are perceived by others, I suggest that such instruments can be used productively by virtually any type of organization.

Personality Testing

Later in my Agency career, I became a certified MBTI assessor, but I don't consider myself an expert. For that reason, I am relying on supplemental insights in this section from Deborah Singer Dobson, a vice president of human resources and coauthor of *Managing Up!* (1999), who has been a certified Myers-Briggs consultant since 1989. Katharine Cook Briggs and her daughter, Isabel Briggs Myers, began developing their Type Indicator for the military during World War II, as women entered the workforce in droves to support the war effort. A fundamental purpose was to provide individuals and management with a tool to determine which jobs people were best suited for.

Deborah notes that Myers-Briggs helps the applicants themselves develop a sense of where they will be most productive and derive the most satisfaction. Myers-Briggs testing can often enable individuals to find their most suitable line of work and develop their capacity to take on leadership roles. HR Solutions head Kevin Sheridan, mentioned earlier in this chapter, agrees with Deborah wholeheartedly that "Myers-Briggs is a perfect example of a . . . pre-employment test that will help you determine whether or not the person has the personality profile of a leader."

I do want to make it clear that the Agency is not necessarily as concerned as companies tend to be about whether individuals can be leaders. The Agency is not looking solely for leaders, but for individuals who can carry out the tasks of a case officer or analyst. They may or may not rise to managerial or executive ranks. The policy of respecting someone for doing a job well, without a sense that the job is a step up the organizational ladder, has served us well.

I also want to draw a distinction between a "good manager," as a generic term describing someone who handles time and resources well, and a "manager," who has reached a level in a company high enough to earn that title. Companies typically draw their leaders from the ranks of managers, which often include people who are "good managers" and should remain managers. MBTI can help both the employee and the company make such a distinction.

Since the Agency doesn't disclose the type of testing it does on candidates for the NCS, I use the MBTI as a foundation for suggesting how such a test could give specific insights into the personality traits of officers and leaders. To begin, the four contrasting aspects of personality are the following—and keep in mind that this is the 30,000-foot view of a nuanced assessment:

1. *Introvert/Extrovert* (I/E): Where is your energy directed—inward or outward? You are more likely to find Agency analysts who are introverts and case officers who are extroverts, though not always. There are strong introverts who have done well as case officers and strong extroverts who have performed well as analysts.

2. *Intuitive/Sensing* (N/S): Here, you see a strong sense of intuition versus attention to detail and precision. The person from your marketing department is more likely to be intuitive while the person from engineering is more likely to be sensing detail. In the Agency, you find case officers that fall into both categories.

3. *Thinking/Feeling* (T/F): The distinction reveals an analytical approach to decision making versus a focus on right/wrong or black/white. The latter may appear to be emotional, but it isn't necessarily. In a discussion of abortion, for example, the thinking person would ask, "Is this early or late term?" or "What are the circumstances?" whereas the feeling person would be driven by a sense of whether or not it's a moral practice.

4. *Judging/Perceiving* (J/P): The judge is quick to conclude something, whereas the perceiver sees possibilities and is open to them.

To a great extent, the names themselves suggest the basic differences: the tendency to look inward (I) or outward (E); to focus on the interpretation or meaning of things (N) or on the basic information (S); to go to logic as a default posture (T) or to focus more on people and the exception to the rule (F); and to move straight toward a decision (J) or to stay open to possible variations (P).

The "leadership types" tend to be ISTJ, INTJ, ESTJ, and ENTJ. This is not to say that having the profile is always predictive of where the person will end up in an organization, but a wealth of statistics does back up the assertion that leaders often fall into one of these categories. And leaders in organizations aren't always people with that title—that's important to keep in mind. There are formal and informal leaders, with some of the informal leaders fitting the MBTI profile I've described, but not in possession of a title that gives them any official authority to lead in an organization. Someone hired yesterday for a junior position could become someone to whom others soon look for guidance; expect to see that person make changes and use his distinction regardless of where the individual sits in the organizational chart.

The fact that we may know a little about the personality profile of a leader does not diminish the complexity of understanding why a person secures a title and position of leadership in a company. Are these people leaders because society rewards the type of behavior they tend to display? Or, because these personality types are more driven? Or, because those people got there first, suggesting that there is a certain amount of clone hiring or clone promoting?

Traits valued by the chief executives—and this is no different from the traits of people who make good case officers in the NCS—might be described as:

* Ability to model

* Ability to execute

The *ability to model* refers to strategic vision, or the relatively easy grasp of what the big picture is. But where are the people with this knack in either the Agency or in private companies? A Gallup poll shows that we have a dearth of strategic leaders. The reason? Leaders who primarily focus on execution tend to rate strategic leaders low, whether in formal reviews through a 360-degree process or informally in the way they treat each other.

Here's the real surprise, though. Strategic leaders rate other strategic leaders low as well. If you have all these models out there to show how the company should look and where it should go, to whom will you look to turn those visions into reality? Someone who can *execute*. This sets up a situation in which it becomes difficult for strategic people to rise very high in an organization—not enough people value them.

Deborah Dobson, for example, has a unique perspective on the concept of "a spy in business" and where the concepts of "leader" and "officer" might diverge. One the projects she examined was led by a retired case officer. He exhibited all the traits of someone accustomed to working independently and reaping rewards for individual success: unilateral decisions, disregard for opinions that didn't jibe with his, and the kind of bluntness that undermined any sense of team. In apologizing for his leadership style, he said he was just doing what he'd learned had worked before. The big difference, of course, was that he had applied that style to leading his individual missions, and in a larger sense, leading his own career. In other words, he had only ever applied it to himself.

Focus on four major breakpoints to make the determination of whether or not your "officer" is predisposed and conditioned to become a "leader." The individual has to be able to do all of the following:

- Give up a certain amount of self (to be able to delegate, set vision, and help other people develop their goals)

- Manage managers

- Manage functions

- Manage businesses

Behavioral Interviewing

Judging individual leadership characteristics inevitably leads to a different type of testing, done in the context of behavioral interviewing. A *behavioral interview* places the candidate in a hypothetical situation to see how the person plays the situation out in her head. This is not role-playing, but rather a decision-making and problem-solving exercise that engages the person in the kinds of subjects and situations that will occur in the job.

One example of behavioral questioning is to ask the candidate to provide an example of a project that went awry, that went off track: "Did you get it back on track? How did you get it back on track? What was the result?" You can start with this exercise using a specific example from the person's career history and then move to a hypothetical situation that relates to the challenges the person will face in the new environment.

Another approach to explore in a behavioral interview invites strategic thinking: "Did you ever set a goal that you didn't achieve? Why not?" You can then do a kind of debriefing with the person to examine if it was an ill-conceived goal not worth achieving or if failure to achieve the goal could have been avoided.

A leader has to connect with other people, as well as manage things. The behavioral interview can help you measure people skills and determine whether or not the candidate can communicate effectively—and, remember, part of communication is listening.

The behavioral interview is also a way to uncover a person's decision-making style. For this, you want to get organization-specific: Does the person's decision-making style mesh with your organization? I know of a technology industry trade group in Washington, D.C., whose long-time executive director had a consensus-building approach to decision making. The concept implies harmony and compromise; it means that everyone walks out of the room agreeing to support the decision, even if it isn't considered ideal by everyone.

When this director retired, the board replaced him with a former three-star general, whose decision-making style was way at the other end of the decision-making spectrum. He issued orders and expected people to follow them. The abrupt change in style was too much for some of the employees, especially the senior ones, who had enjoyed contributing to decisions and had come to see that as a matter of respect. Several of them immediately began looking for other positions. In an ideal world, the board would have looked at the hazards, as well as the positives, in such a dramatic shift in style. But just like voters in congressional and presidential elections, sometimes eliminating the status quo is all anyone focuses on.

In *Rangers Lead the Way*, Dean Hohl (2003) does a great job of summarizing the types of decision-making styles, as follows:

- *"I tell; you do."* That was the general's style. Works very well when you're short on time, short on independent thinking and/or competence on your team, and there are clear lines of authority.

- *"Here is my decision. What are your critical concerns?"* Someone who uses the first one might move to this more inclusive style if he has time to listen or has been coached to make others feel as though they have something to contribute.

- *"I haven't made up my mind yet. I'd like your input."* As you move to the midpoint on the spectrum, you need more competence in your team, and in some cases more time, in order to effect sound decisions. "

- *"Majority rules."* The bad part of this style is that the "majority" may be only one person more than the other side has.

- *"Consensus required."* This approach is time-consuming because the level of participation is high and there is no decision until everyone agrees. Nevertheless, with a group of competent people, this is a good route to an enduring decision. Experts often use this style in designing industry standards, whether it's technology, construction, or the composition of paint.

- *"Delegated decision."* This style is fast, but desirable only when the person designated to make the decision is competent and experienced.

Even people who look like they might be good leaders may never get there, for one important reason: Moving into a leadership role is not a competence shift, it's a value shift. You can be extremely gifted in dealing with people, but if it's in your nature to go it alone, and you want all of the recognition and reward yourself, then you are not going to be an effective leader.

When I returned to Headquarters after almost twenty years in the field as a case officer, there was no guarantee that I would fit on any floor at Langley, much less on the top floor. Or was there? The tests I took earlier in my career may have suggested that I would transition well from individual contributor to leader, but the Agency doesn't base a decision to promote someone to the level of executive on those tests, any more than a private company would. Virtually all Agency decisions to promote individuals to more senior positions are based on the evaluations they received for their various assignments and the judgments or assessments of their seniors. The major value of testing at the Agency, then, is to help an individual with self-awareness. As a corollary, the tests might also serve to validate a recommendation to promote based on someone's performance.

* * *

Behavioral interviewing, personality testing, and track record help an organization determine who has leadership potential, as well as to weed out the people who should never be brought to C-suites—or even to desks reserved for managers. Just as important, standardized tests help individuals be clear on their own abilities and preferences in their work environment.

Officer	Leader
High-end individual contributor	High-end individual contributor who can drop focus on self to focus on others
Ability to see big picture	Ability to see big picture and communicate it to others
Ability to execute	Ability to execute and create situation where others can also execute

MAKING THE CUT

Most organizations cannot function without the people who do the day-to-day stuff. They are vital to the functioning of the Agency as much as any other type of business. There is nothing "less than" about employees who show up promptly at 9:00 AM every day, work diligently, and look forward to every fifteen-minute break and two-week vacation. So when I talk in Chapter 4 about having a workforce of engaged employees, I don't exclude the people who have no aspirations of becoming leaders or managers. By this I mean that it is not only officers—or whatever you call top performers—who are worth company-wide appreciation. Even in the NCS, the Agency hires individuals in any number of specialty categories to exercise their unique skills, though not necessarily to become case officers.

The Agency would never knowingly hire someone less than a top candidate to serve as a case officer—that is, a person who will carry out clandestine operations. There are many reasons, however, why you might want people who are not so-called top performers in a company—for positions other than those requiring independent thinking, good judgment, perseverance, and self-confidence. In hiring these people, you should be sure that you don't set them on a career path, or a promotion path, along which they will need to be high-end individual contributors or leaders in order to survive. If you do so, you are setting them up for failure.

After spotting the criteria discussed earlier, the Agency looks for people who have demonstrated that they can cooperate. This is another way of saying, "Choose people you want in your sandbox, not those who try to bully their way into it." It doesn't matter how smart or accomplished a person is; a top performer is only good on a team if that person can share a passion for accomplishing a common mission. A top performer who is not a team player can disrupt the team dynamic. Finally, the Agency avoids hiring someone whose default response to something going wrong is to blame someone or something else. These people with a victim mentality will find a way to poison your operations.

At the heart of Kevin Sheridan's "magnetic culture," described earlier in this chapter, are "engaged employees"—that is, mentally energized people who are committed to realizing the mission and living the values of the organization. Research by HR Solutions shows you can characterize these people as:

- Loyal

- Motivated

- Committed

- Driven by their job content

- An inspiration to others; positive people

- Optimistic

- Supportive of coworkers

- Oriented to providing good customer service

Beyond trying to find people with these qualities, the Agency does have some expectations that do not necessarily apply in business, although they would be beneficial, depending on the position. Primarily, we look for individuals who can process information quickly. We don't need to recruit from the ranks of Mensa, where some of the brightest might also be overtly plodding in their decision making as they consider every angle of a problem. The Agency looks for street-smart people: those able to ascertain conditions, consider options, and move quickly. There are no "school solutions" to many of the tasks that Clandestine officers undertake. On the contrary, there is a great deal of ad hoc contingency planning to support impromptu action. The challenges these decision makers face are fast-breaking, so their minds have to be able to sort through options at lightning speed.

But then, many people in sales, as well as in professions such as emergency medicine and law enforcement, would say the same thing about their personnel.

HIRING TO SUPPORT YOUR MISSION

A *promising* candidate does the following, at the very least:

- Researches the company, its people, and its competition

- Comes to interviews prepared to apply that research

- Talks straight; does not exaggerate in describing previous accomplishments

- Tests straight; does not try to second-guess the tests and interviewers

- Demonstrates a sense of personal responsibility—that is, does not habitually blame others for missteps and failures

A *very desirable* candidate also does the following:

- Has compelling reasons for wanting to join the organization

- Communicates how her core strengths align with those needed for the position

A *high-potential* candidate also does the following:

- Demonstrates his talents and skills without losing sight of how other people fit into achieving a goal

- Sees the big picture and knows how to share the view with others, as appropriate, to get the job done

- Takes timely action to meet demands and helps others to do the same

CHAPTER FOUR

Building a Committed Cadre

Hiring people with the right qualities does very little for your organization in the long run unless you actively keep those people engaged. They need to sense that their work is truly valued.

As I noted earlier, recruitment is the heart of what case officers do at the Agency. The nature of the work is engaging and Headquarters makes sure that work can be carried on by providing ongoing training and mentoring. If a case officer needs to influence the media in a particular country, for example, he gets familiar with their professional terrain and then tries to recruit people in those media. The case officer's stratagem for working his way into their network and putting people in play in that network keeps him sharp and interested, day after day. Discussing the challenges of the task with colleagues keeps everyone connected to the overarching mission.

Many men and women enjoy corporate life as much as spies appreciate their clandestine lives, but there are a lot more people out there who don't get excited about going to work every day. The cost to the American economy of *not* building an engaged workforce is $350 billion annually, according to recent numbers from Gallup. That's not a typo. If you translate that statistic roughly into days of productivity lost owing to nonperformance, the conclusions are staggering. No one would be satisfied if the local grocery store were open only four out of every seven days, yet that is akin to the diminished potential we face with nonperformance. Another interpretation of this loss of economic activity comes from hard data collected by Gallup, HR Solutions, and others: Disengaged employees drag operating margins down; engaged employees pump them up. There is no middle ground on that statement.

Part of this economic cost is turnover, but part of it is the hidden costs of employee apathy or outright discontent. HR Solutions' research shows that 59 percent of working people are "quit and stay" employees—that is, they collect their paychecks regularly, but do the minimum required to earn those paychecks. They get their checks every couple of weeks, but they "quit" their jobs years ago. They are also known as the clock-watchers—people who come in late every once in a while and stay late only if they receive a financial incentive to do so. When there is an opportunity to volunteer for something, these are the people who bow their heads in the hope they aren't called on. The *CIA Factbook* puts the total number of American workers at about 150 million, so the 59 percent who are quit-and-stay employees translates roughly to 88.5 million people who are doing a good job of slowing down the economy. The productive employees—the people who promote the brand and expend extra effort—make up less than 40 percent of the workforce.

FOSTERING EMPLOYEE ENGAGEMENT

Agency statistics on employment and productivity don't match those of corporate America. With a much higher proportion of engaged employees, and far fewer than the 59 percent national average of quit-and-stay employees, the Agency holds some solutions for corporate America. Key reasons for its superior percentages are the training and education opportunities that are omnipresent during the careers of case officers. (I talk about these programs later in this chapter.) The foundation for solid employee engagement, and the reasons the training and education are effective, have been researched by HR Solutions. The key drivers for getting and keeping employees engaged are a healthy management relationship and good prospects for career advancement, as well as a sense of genuine accomplishment—that is, making a real contribution to the national security of the country.

Before I explore those factors, though, let's consider what it's like to work for a company that has earned the title "Best Employer in America." *Fortune* magazine annually lists the best places to work, after conducting what the magazine states as "the most extensive employee survey in corporate America." In 2009, that survey involved more than 81,000 employees at 353 companies. (Note: In the magazine's survey of graduating MBAs, both public- and private-sector employers are ranked, with the CIA consistently making the top 100.) NetApp, a Sunnyvale, California, technology company, rose to the top of the list, for a number of reasons, including policies that reflect what *Fortune* called a "down-to-earth management ethos" and an innovative approach to planning, in which business units write "future histories" to describe what their operations will look like a couple of years down the road. The management ethos characterizes a healthy management–employee relationship that surfaces in many ways, such as reasonable and flexible policies regarding travel and telecommuting—policies that show the company respects the judgments of its employees. The planning approach invites employees to be visionaries and, in a real way, is another way of saying, "To some extent, you can chart your own destiny here." Embedded in that approach is a strong sense of career advancement—after all, what talented employees would create a "future history" that documents a career to nowhere?

Now let's take a closer look at the two factors.

A Healthy Management Relationship

Leon Panetta, current director of the Central Intelligence Agency, handed out earplugs to his case officers in Iraq so they could block out the political squabbling in Washington about their work. They got the sense he knows how they feel being criticized for doing their job. In the spring of 2009, just after he took over as director, Panetta flew nearly 30,000 miles to meet in person with case officers and other CIA employees in the field. Just showing up and listening must have infused a positive spirit into their relationship with the new management at Langley.

A commanding officer has to be respectful, trustworthy, and a good communicator who sets clear expectations. Those qualities elicit loyalty and commitment, and they draw people to an organization and help reinforce their links to it. The opposite is true, too. *Psychology Today* (Lawson, 2005) reported the results of a Gallup poll that indicated "a bad relationship with the boss is the number one reason for quitting a job. Supervisor problems outplace all other areas of worker dissatisfaction, including salary, work hours or day-to-day duties. And employees leave supervisors, not companies."

It's very difficult for a new field operations officer to hit the tarmac running. For most of us, including me, it takes a while to hit our stride. The benefits of being mentored by people who have done it for a number of years cannot be underestimated. When I was a junior officer in the field, my colleagues were almost all older and more experienced than I was, and they went to great lengths to mentor me on doing clandestine operations. Technically speaking, they weren't "bosses," but they did represent management by virtue of their seniority. They were particularly helpful in guiding me on the best ways to meet and develop contacts abroad. Without the insights of professionals who had been around the block—literally, since they knew the geography and I didn't, as well as figuratively— building new relationships of possible operational interest would have been a daunting challenge. And as I encountered operational situations, such as trying to understand people's motivations, I always talked over my cases with these senior colleagues. My learning from them was a bit like a resident doctor in a hospital, developing a diagnosis technique and treatment options through Grand Rounds. In the process, they could always see where I was in my personal development and what next steps I was establishing. Having such strong relationships with these senior case officers paid off in the higher quality of my work and the greater output at the station, as well as providing me with emotional support. There's no question that their mentoring contributed to a healthy Agency–worker relationship.

The Agency institutionalized this mentoring process to some extent by assigning senior people to guide junior officers. These people weren't necessarily direct supervisors; instead, we junior officers benefited from assigned matches based on roles and personalities.

A healthy management relationship involves both parties contributing, of course. It isn't all give, give, give on the part of senior individuals, with new or less experienced persons absorbing the information and wisdom. The assumption should be that both people have something to give each other. When I was the director of media relations, I had an immediate subordinate who had been both a journalist and worked in the public affairs office. He served as a tremendous resource for me, sharing his experiences with the media and bolstering my ability to do my job.

CEOs who understand the importance of having healthy relationships with employees—no matter how many of them there are—do the things you see recommended in those management guidebooks: they walk the floor of the manufacturing plant, go on sales calls every once in a while, meet casually with different departments. Some of them go way beyond the recommendations, though, and that pays off in both financial and emotional rewards.

Nucor is a steel and steel-products company with annual sales of $23.7 billion and net income of $1.8 billion. The company's track record in average return on capital and growth has earned it a place repeatedly among *BusinessWeek's* (2009) 50 Best Performers. But it's how Nucor has accomplished these impressive returns and growth during a severe economic downturn that makes the company worth profiling. Having no layoffs and offering a creative compensation program have helped prepare the company for the economic turnaround; and in the meantime, it was able to push productivity up, even though total pay went down. It is one of those rare examples of a corporate mission statement coming to life. On the company's Web site, the first line of that statement is "Nucor Corporation is made up of approximately 20,000 teammates." With a focus on keeping the company moving forward by treating those 20,000 employees like teammates, CEO Daniel DiMicco and COO John Ferriola have received thank-you e-mails and cards by the hundreds. It took ingenuity and commitment on the part of the "teammates," and not just the team leaders, to make things move when the orders stopped coming in or were cancelled. People who used to work on the manufacturing line, and whose compensation was tied to the productivity of that line, plunged into non-manufacturing tasks, many of which came about through their suggestions. To "earn their keep," they started mowing the lawn, cleaning the bathrooms, and doing general maintenance around the buildings, as well as rewriting manuals and brainstorming for ways to cut costs.

One of the broad lessons of the Nucor story is, "Don't trash your talent in a downturn." As described earlier, the cost of hiring a good employee includes a great deal of human effort and monetary investment that companies make readily in times of prosperity. When things turn sour economically, though, people often find out about their layoffs in an e-mail. But if they were brilliant a year ago, when the company had great quarterly returns, they are probably still brilliant when the company's income slips. The C-level employees need to make that clear to the rest of the organization through their actions.

The Agency is not immune to economic downturns, but its downturn is more likely to result from a perceived diminution in threats to the country's national security, such as happened at the end of the Cold War in 1991, when the Soviet Union ceased to exist. A similar situation occurred in the 1970s with the end of the Vietnam War, at which time the Agency underwent the highly publicized pink-slip exercise known as "The Halloween Massacre." That is, after increasing its ranks during the build-up to and involvement in the Vietnam War, the Agency abruptly faced the need to downsize. CIA Director Bill Colby realized the problem, but left it to his successor, Director of Central Intelligence (DCI) Stansfield Turner, to carry out the reductions in force. Unfortunately, the job was poorly done, resulting in widespread anger among the workforce, including those who had not been selected out.

At the end of the Cold War, the Agency had another downsizing, reducing stations around the world, as well as letting the ranks of the Directorate of Operations decrease through attrition. This force reduction followed the pattern occurring throughout the U.S. government when the Soviet Union collapsed. The State Department, the military, and other agencies concerned with national security all saw decreases in personnel and operations.

Those actions that put people out of work damaged the health of the relationship they had with management in the short term, and sometimes for years to come. You can give grand reasons, like "the war is over" or "it's the economy" to people who are losing their jobs, but they are still losing their jobs. While you may not be able to save everyone from losing her job, much depends on how the dismissal is managed. Recognizing their contributions and facilitating a transition to life beyond the Agency went a long way toward keeping the good-will of persons who had to leave, as well as those who remained. This experience applies to the private sector as much as it did to the Agency.

Whether public agency or private-sector business, managers have all learned that respect for the individual's talents and contributions must be part of the equation, no matter what decisions are made regarding the size of the workforce.

Career Advancement

Becoming an executive is definitely not the objective of most people who serve in the National Clandestine Service (NCS). To us, "career advancement" often means doing something we perceive as central to the mission. Consistent with this take on progress is the fact that training and education have meaning in the context of a person's career and aren't there to serve merely as a change of pace or quasi-entertainment.

This attitude isn't unlike what many corporate employees want, especially now that "climbing the corporate ladder" means little to people whose sense of advancement is defined as becoming a better engineer or graphic artist or investment banker during their time with the company. The path to success for an individual may not be from a cubicle to the office with a window. Success may, instead, be movement from a relatively routine project to a complex one, on which a person can build his reputation. Nevertheless, the commonality in the two perceptions of career advancement is predictability: People want to know that their excellent performance will lead to more satisfying and challenging opportunities.

Companies can learn a lot from the military model of career advancement for officers, which is similar to the Agency's, except that case officers can leave the Agency as easily as anyone in a civilian job. The military model provides people with the knowledge that there is a new challenge coming in a given period of time. After serving for a while in a given job assignment, and perhaps after a certain amount of training and education, an individual may be considered for promotion to a higher position. There is a mutual expectation on the part of the U.S. military and the officer that each will get what's deserved. Because the Agency is part of the federal government, we also have a structure in place for increases in grade level and pay, as well as change of "command." Although the career path may not be quite as predictable as in a military environment, it is easy for a case officer to set expectations regarding career development and advancement. That is not so easy for most corporate executives; at some point, however, that predictability stops.

For example, soon after Judge William Webster was named CIA director, one of the first issues he addressed was succession planning, a subset of "talent management." Regardless of what you call it, the process figures into both of the drivers behind engaged employees. It involves early identification of employees who bring a tremendous amount to the organization, and it involves connecting with people who can provide mentoring and opportunities. Companies have finally realized the value in devoting resources to determine which new employees should be mentored, trained, and educated, with advancement to the top management tier as the potential career agenda.

ONBOARDING

The process of engaging a newly hired person starts with *onboarding*, a core concept of employee engagement that is integral to the development of a "magnetic culture," as described by HR Solutions founder Kevin Sheridan. It aptly describes what happens when someone first joins the NCS.

The onboarding process is what used to be called "new employee orientation," but it goes far beyond that. It used to be that the orientation process involved filling out forms for the IRS, health insurance, and a retirement account. Then the human resources person, or maybe your boss or someone in administration, would escort you to your desk and you would start working. What an inspiring welcome! Now the construct is different.

Many private companies know what the Agency knew earlier, only because of its mission-related requirements: Getting someone on board involves emotions, not just paperwork. You can't sit someone at a desk that has a top drawer stuffed with random printouts, and expect that the material won't bother that individual. You can't expect someone to feel part of the operation if everyone else has a badge that allows entry all over campus, but she has only a paste-on nametag. I know a senior editor at a major publishing house in New York who, for twenty days following her hiring, had to go through the same security procedure as visitors go through; it took that long for someone in the company's HR department to get her the credentials she needed to walk into the building and take the elevator.

Here's a chilling fact, collected from the extensive survey work of HR Solutions: One out of every twenty-five employees quits on the first day.

It's not that odd, if you put yourself in the mind and heart of the individual who took that job. The new manager makes an attempt to bond with the candidate. Promises fly—on both sides. Expectations are high. And then there is immediate and severe disappointment. All that candidate wants is reassurance that she made the right decision, and all she gets is red flags that this company has no respect for its employees.

The worst-case scenario for companies—the one that underlies the statistic just mentioned—is a result of one or more of the following:

- The boss is not there on the first day to provide a welcome and orientation.

- No one introduces the new worker to coworkers.

- The new hire is led to a cubicle full of dust and the remnants of the previous occupant—half-used memo pad, candy wrappers, sticky paper clips.

- The computer isn't set up, or it's set up and no one gave the new hire the password.

- The voice mail still has the quirky message of the previous employee.

These are all triggers that feed the anxiety of a new employee. And that is why people quit on the first day. The shock of being such a nonentity, of being taken for granted before the first eight hours are even up, often send self-respecting persons out the door for good.

In reality, these things happen on a regular basis to new employees in the Agency, too. We try to hire people who can put such petty obstacles into perspective and get on with their jobs. Our employees cannot be environment dependent, since they often serve under hardship conditions.

Look at your own work environment and consider the relative importance of physical setting. If you want someone to work in your organization, install the incentives that will keep the individual there from the moment he walks in the door. And don't forget to take the person to lunch to celebrate the alliance.

Engagement levels change during an employee's life cycle with the organization. Within a month, new employees can become less engaged, and this disengagement slide is what you have to combat during the onboarding process.

TRAINING AND/OR EDUCATION

I see training and education as totally different disciplines. Training focuses on building skills. I can train you to type. I can train you to drive. I can train you to shoot. In contrast, education provides opportunity for intellectual growth; it helps cultivate insights that lead to stronger performance in your profession. If education has anything to do with typing, driving, or shooting, it's only how to best apply those skills to accomplish a mission.

If you've landed a job that you can do well immediately, then the chances are you are in a dead-end position in terms of your career. Case officers go from station to station essentially doing the same job: recruiting agents. Software engineers go from project to project or company to company doing the same job: designing and developing software systems. In each case, for professional development to occur, either the level or the type of challenge has to change with each new assignment. And if the company wants you to succeed, then you will get the training and education you need to progress. Using the excuse that the job is merely a stepping-stone to a position with real growth works for a short while, but we all know employees who use that excuse, year after year. The regular paycheck makes them complacent.

Employees should look forward to training, and companies should take their training programs seriously. Good training helps cultivate a high-performance workforce and strengthens an organization overall. Training is not only about employee preparedness to take on competitive challenges but also about building the organizational culture. Likewise, employees should look forward to education, which will impart deep knowledge of both their careers and their chosen industry. As I explain later in this chapter, in my stint as chief of executive development in the Agency's Office of Training and Education, I believed that it was essential to expose officers to ideas and perspectives they would not ordinarily get in the course of their work.

Continuous training and continuing education help avoid what industry analysts at Gartner Inc. have dubbed the "hype cycle"—the rise of performance expectations after the introduction of a new technology, followed by a slump into disillusionment and then a modest rise to a plateau of productivity. In practical terms, if the organization doesn't support the change, then the change will not occur.

Through the extended and intensive process of interviewing, testing, and initial training of new hires, the Agency leads a candidate to feel special if she has made the cut. The secrecy associated with the career and the mentoring from veterans of field operations, training in tradecraft, investment in development of language skills, exposure to new cultures and dangerous situations, and opportunities to take breaks from the routine and explore new ideas and processes—all of these factors reinforce that sense of feeling special. In a real sense, the Agency system of bringing people into the Clandestine Service, as well as keeping them there, is designed to avoid that "hype cycle."

CONTINUOUS TRAINING

The Agency looks at training as continuing throughout the course of a career. Private organizations that support ongoing training also demonstrate an appreciation for professional development. They want employees to be able to add a dimension to their contributions to the organization. A person may be a regional sales representative today, but with additional training in presentation skills, technology forecasting, financial analysis, budgeting, risk management, or similar specialties, he will be able to advance on his career track. Continuous training reflects what an employee needs to know for meeting current, day-to-day responsibilities, as well as what the person needs to know later as he advances in the company.

An employee needs specialized training to operate in the job and generalized training to relate effectively with people who perform complementary, supervisory, or support roles. In the Agency, we train to develop both hard and soft skills; I begin here with the soft skills, as they are more transferable to business.

Soft-skills training is the type of training that seems to get cut first, though, isn't it? Obviously, that's a mistake. The common reason for cutting this kind of training is that, once the company has someone on board, that person has a job to do and collects a good paycheck for doing it, so why bother to train for a skill that doesn't address bottom-line, how-to issues? Indeed, some executives think the paycheck should be incentive enough for a person to perform at 100 percent and get things done harmoniously with coworkers. Executives have to counter that bias by citing the overwhelming evidence indicating that "reading" people, "managing" conversations, matching decision-making styles to the team makeup, and other so-called soft skills have a marked effect on productivity and employee satisfaction. And higher productivity and greater employee satisfaction ultimately mean that the company makes more money.

Another budget cut that makes no sense is eliminating the proactive steps to check with employees and find out where they stand with the organization. Are they engaged? Just asking the question once a month, every month, helps cultivate greater interest and enhanced ability to contribute. Kevin Sheridan says, "I've run into thousands of organizations in my twenty years as an engagement specialist that make myopic decisions to cut the employee survey, cut the recognition program, cut the training program—they think of it as 'soft-skill, HR junk'—and those knee-jerk reactions don't consider the hard cost of disengaging employees."

Soft-skills continuous training is most easily done via several of the following ways.

Storytelling

John Wooden, a Basketball Hall of Famer as both a player and a college coach unsurpassed for NCAA championships, earned a reputation for annoying his players by having them practice free throws. But then, it was one of many of his coaching techniques that worked, season after season. And so, in giving you this short section on storytelling, just think of me as John Wooden. I'm telling you to practice something you need to be good at because, when it really counts, you had better be able to deliver.

When the 2009 listing of *Fortune* 500 companies appeared, I expected to breeze through lists of expected companies ranked by size and within industries. Instead, the pages that caught my eye listed six minority suppliers. It was story after story of how people belonging to minority groups in America had created impressive business success. I didn't realize until I'd finished the piece that this was an advertising section, not a news article. The descriptions were of sons of Cuban exiles, and a former cop who had been wounded in the line of duty; I was moved by their accomplishments. Would I seek out their services or products if I had a need for them? That's certainly more likely, now that I knew their stories.

True stories can profoundly influence behavior and are primary vehicles for training and education. People rarely remember exactly what a trainer says (or what's written in a book), but they will remember how what a trainer said made them feel. That is the real impact of storytelling. Stories about individuals in your organization who performed in outstanding ways can impart a sense of pride to new employees—it says that the organization develops and recognizes individuals. The story of Captain Chesley "Sully" Sullenberger, who landed his commercial airplane in the Hudson River, comes to mind. Reportedly, he checked the passenger cabin a couple of times to ensure that all passengers and crew had evacuated before he left the sinking aircraft himself. Surely his company, US Airways, and his professional colleagues were proud of him; they felt his performance reflected well on his skills as an aviator, as well as the overall standards of performance of the airline. That kind of story might well inspire other pilots to refresh their water-landing skills and other emergency procedures.

Storytelling affects the way people in the world conduct business, interact socially, and even write laws. Some of the most memorable examples of storytelling's role in history come from the annals of propaganda, though you could term this negative storytelling. Rather than boosting pride, it is storytelling to incite action by instilling fear. That is, when countries go to war, they publicize the atrocities of the enemy to dehumanize them. They tell stories about how horrible the enemy can be so that an entire population will want to take action against them. *The Protocols of the Elders of Zion* is one such example—a pack of lies that continues to haunt the world. By concocting stories about a Jewish conspiracy to take over the world, a Russian named Pyotr Rachovsky created a reason for action: The widespread discontent in Russia had its roots in something other than the czar's repression of the populace. Since their first appearance in 1903, *The Protocols* have been reprinted, publicized, and even taught in school. Adolf Hitler used them as a basis for his campaign against the Jews, and the stories continue as the source of anti-Semitic propaganda today.

On the positive side, museums in communities both large and small document the stories of local and national heroes. In fact, museums contribute to both the cultural life and the spirit of those communities by illustrating the stories of heroism and accomplishment in displays and reenactments. Schoolchildren make field trips to places like the Smithsonian's Air & Space Museum in Washington, D.C., and some come away with dreams they realize many years later when they get a degree in astrophysics. Or they come to the International Spy Museum, and a decade later they are filling out an application to become an officer in the National Clandestine Service.

In terms of training, stories serve to illustrate how-to information in memorable ways. In terms of education, they give insights into pivotal decisions and provide a context for understanding how the organization has succeeded and failed in providing value to its constituents. Sometimes stories do nothing more than reinforce a sense of connection to other people who've done the same job, but that connection should not be underrated if it builds pride. The U.S. Marine Corps makes effective use of storytelling for this purpose, if you look at their Web site or visit the Marine Corps Museum in Quantico, Virginia. The museum is very much a story-driven institution, as is the Corps itself.

When I went through Marine boot camp in the 1950s, our drill instructors were all young noncommissioned officers (NCOs) recently returned from combat in Korea. In between calling for more pushups and running us around the parade ground at port arms, they fed us a steady diet of war stories from the front, emphasizing how weak and puny our efforts were compared to the men they had served with in combat. Their questioning of whether any of us would ever qualify to become real Marines was a constant challenge. And the stories were always vivid, complete with names and colorful descriptions—just like the Marines who raised the flag on Mount Surabachi on Iwo Jima. Semper Fi! The Corps story is burned into every young man and woman until each, too, comes to believe he has become an honored member of a warrior band dating back to the earliest days of the republic. The magic is in the stories.

The use of stories to reinforce the connection to the Agency and to the heroes of the Agency is much like that of the stories told by military, sports teams, and other groups that have powerful shared experiences. In some cases, they lead to traditions that once had a story behind them but now have a life of their own—for example, the ritual of the "rally cap," when players sit in the dugout with their hats on inside out during a rally.

An Agency tradition that stays tied to a particular story involves Nathan Hale. The CIA's Nathan Hale statue stands in front of the original Headquarters building and is occasionally used as a meeting site. It's common to find quarters placed in the metal ropes that bind Hale's hands, or perhaps on his shoes. When the British hanged Hale as a spy during the Revolutionary War, he declared his regret that he had only one life to give for his country—a message that has inspired others who pursue the craft of espionage in wartime. The quarters are reminders of the man who invited and needed Hale's service—George Washington, whose face appears on the coin.

Stories that reinforce the Agency's emphasis on continuing training and education often appear in the publication *Studies in Intelligence*, the "Journal of the American Intelligence Professional," which has both classified and unclassified versions. Examples of the stories that illustrate specific how-tos are George G. Bull's article on elicitation techniques that appeared in the fall 1970 issue (and was classified "secret" at the time and a long while afterward), and W. J. McKee's spring 1983 article on issues of quality related to writing reports from the field. (McKee's work was also classified "secret" when first published, and when reprinted in H. Bradfield Westerfield's *Inside CIA's Private World* [1995], with portions still redacted.)

George Bull was serving in West Germany when he decided to document the practice of elicitation in the recruitment process for his fellow case officers. He examined the "practical problems" that officers in the field face in collecting human intelligence, or HUMINT. He logged the five main problems as (1) finding a reason to talk to the source, (2) locating the source, (3) positively identifying the person as the one you want, (4) maintaining cover during the encounter, and (5) keeping the source focused on the subject you want to discuss. And then, using his stories from the field, he elaborated on how to get the job done. Although a lot of people who serve as case officers today could have written the article, he's the one who actually did, and his stories contributed to the training of new and junior officers who followed him.

In W. J. McKee's piece, he addressed fundamental issues of objectivity and quality in a field report and, even though portions of his article are redacted, we still get the how-to message. His article serves as a good training piece on identifying bias in a report, and on looking at the mechanics of providing material that is reliable, authenticated, and accurate. One of McKee's stories that makes the information stick is related to speed versus accuracy. McKee told of locking horns with a U.S. Cabinet officer over the way to transmit sensitive and timely information; since the information pertained directly to negotiations the Cabinet member was conducting that day, McKee just picked up the phone.

Some companies invest similarly in trying to record the lore and stories of company founders and key contributors, but many do not. In a few cases, extremely high-profile CEOs like Jack Welch have packaged the lore in their memoirs, which become recommended reading for employees. Welch also made a point of attending GE's seminars for its rising young professionals and sparring with them in town hall-type settings—a vivid way to reinforce the practical value of the stories he told. He regarded his participation as a key aspect of his leadership role. Executives like Virgin Atlantic Airways founder Sir Richard Branson take that a notch higher by accomplishing extraordinary feats outside the work environment—so the company's employees become "adventurers by association," with the company itself identifying to an extent with the feats of its colorful leader.

The primary impact of stories may be their conveying a sense of "this is how we do business." The collection and writing of these stories should be done consciously, rather than randomly, to keep the information accurate. Many companies take a somewhat fragmentary approach to this by using their Web pages to contain news articles and press releases, thereby serving as the repository of corporate stories. Those stories are fine for the outside world, but if an executive wants to cultivate a corporate culture and educate the workforce, the company must invest the talent in its communications department to produce stories that explain both successes and exemplary failures.

Company stories are an inescapable, and enjoyable, part of doing business with the Charles Machine Works, also known as the "Ditch Witch" company. It seems as though there's never a boring answer to any question about the organization, from why the company is in Perry, Oklahoma, to how a trencher came to be called "Ditch Witch" to why it's orange. I heard about the company from Jim McCormick, who had been a keynote speaker at both an international-dealer sales meeting and an international-dealer service meeting. "The stories make people feel connected," he said. "They help engender a sense that the company and its business partners are a community with a shared heritage and memories." Some of the stories made their way into *The First Generation*, a book by Fred Beers that is part of a series documenting the pioneering spirit of Oklahoma; it gives you the distinct impression that many Oklahomans, no matter what they do for a living, feel like the Ditch Witch stories belong to them, too.

Charlie Malzahn, a blacksmith, founded the company, but it was his son Ed who invented the Ditch Witch. Ed had a curiosity about machines and tools that would not quit. At two years old, he lost three fingers on his left hand in an accident in his father's shop. That's didn't stop him from experimenting with tools, even though it did make him ineligible many years later for military service. By the age of thirteen, he had built lots of innovations. After reading a book on castings, he made an impression of a silver dollar in a plaster mold and manufactured fake coins that he hand-ed out to his friends at school. Federal authorities paid a friendly visit and broke the mold. They came back a few years later when Ed mounted a spotlight on the top of the family garage and used a remote-control to shine it on neighbors and airplanes. Unfortunately, Army Air Force pilots practiced night flying at nearby Vance Field, and the federal government had concerns that the spotlight belonged to a spy.

Armed with a mechanical engineering degree, Ed invented the Ditch Witch in 1948, after watching a couple of employees of a local plumber hand-dig a shallow trench with picks and shovels. His basic concept was to put a bunch of shovel heads on a chain and he refined the idea from there. He developed a low-cost trenching machine with those plumbers helpers in mind—something that could rip through dense Oklahoma clay.

One of the top ten questions that visitors to the company's facility ask is, "Why are Ditch Witch trenchers orange?" Ed's story is that he had been painting one of the company's other products red to try to hide the black iron and call attention to its use as a safety tool. The red paint did not do a good job, though, and Ed blamed the man who had sold him the paint. The man gave him another brand and the same problem occurred, so in frustration, he gave him a can of orange paint and said, "Try this." It worked better. When the Ditch Witch came along, he adopted the orange color for that, too, so he wouldn't have to clean the paint gun twice. So, while the main color of construction equipment was and is yellow, the Ditch Witch remains orange.

What do you get out of the anecdotes about Ed Malzahn? That the company's values include curiosity, competence, and straightforward solutions. And from its earliest days, the company (i.e., father Charlie) encouraged Ed's risk taking, with constant opportunities to get into the shop and use his imagination. Having Jim McCormick speak to the company's dealers drove that point home, since Jim focused on the rewards of taking intelligent risks.

In essence, stories are much more powerful than mission statements, which usually feature abstract concepts and vague words such as *honesty, integrity,* and *diligence.* Stories give life to the concepts because people have put them into action. More than that, stories build a mystique and give richness to a brand that helps form a "magnetic culture."

EXPERIENTIAL LEARNING

Case officers are like broken-field runners in football—always adapting to the changing situation, making split-second decisions on how to complete a play. Practice in making decisions on the spot is embedded in much of the training, therefore, but the decisions are often grounded in basic skills and experiential training that has preceded.

For example, Agency employees may receive language training if they are about to be assigned to a foreign country. *Tradecraft* training is experiential learning for people going into a *denied area,* where they must operate under constant surveillance. (A *denied area* is a term for countries that, from the perspective of the Intelligence service, are considered hostile.)

That is, the country places the employees under close 24/7 surveillance and does everything possible to monitor activities and disrupt operations. The *denied* category used to include the Eastern European countries and now includes countries like Iraq. So, the training involves practicing dead drops and other techniques for surreptitiously passing information, becoming skilled in methods of eluding people who are tailing you, and role-playing to practice interacting in the cover identity.

One type of tradecraft training is driving—one of many disciplines that require physical dexterity and quick decision making. The CIA maintains a fleet of used cars especially for helping operatives hone defensive-driving skills. The value of this training is not only in knowing how to perform physically in the face of a threat but also how to quickly build contingency plans for escape routes, assess the threat level based on knowledge of the attacker, and so on. These mental and physical skills are directly transferable to the less obviously dramatic situations in which case officers find themselves. For example, practice in making life-saving split-second decisions when a suspicious car suddenly heads for you can also prepare you to make both small and significant decisions more agilely than people who have never been tested under pressure.

Precisely the same kind of mental skills training can prepare someone in business for high-caliber decision making when a crisis hits. This is why experiential training programs for potential executives provide some of the best preparation for the big decisions in corporate life. The Wharton Leadership Ventures Program, for example, helps test the leadership capabilities of MBA students by putting them on some of the world's highest mountains, where the consequences of their actions are extreme and immediate. Wharton's MBA students are held accountable for their decisions when faced with uncertainty, with director Preston Kline analyzing the reactions to see if the students' fall-back mechanisms are fight, flight, or freeze. He helps the students understand whether their mechanisms are sustainable in their future roles as business executives.

Former Army Ranger Dean Hohl founded a corporate training program called Leading Concepts (www.leadingconcepts.com), which gives participants the experience of teamwork, leadership, and communication in true Ranger style. The program focuses on mimicking the real and acute challenges of wartime battles, and by doing so, it provides provoking answers to certain questions very quickly, especially those related to personality and circumstances. For example, for personality:

* What are your innate abilities?

* What are your strongest senses?

* How do you perform under pressure?

For circumstances:

* What physical resources are available to you?

* How much time do you have?

* Who's on your side?

* Who wants you to fail?

The high-urgency training exercises are designed to help participants handle workplace "survival situations" with greater efficiency and confidence. In a physical sense, these experiences bear no resemblance to workplace situations; the parallel is in the mutual experience of limited resources, a common objective, and a lot of pressure to get a job done. For instance, Dean takes people into the woods of Kentucky and provides camouflage outfits, prepackaged military meals, an uncomfortable place to sleep, and a paintball gun to protect food, shelter, and body. Four days of missions involve some compelling objectives; for example, if you don't take the supply tent, you don't capture your food for the day. The point is to send people back to their workplaces with a new perspective. Dean gets people to look at their coworkers and realize, "I see you in a new light. I know you better than I did before, even though I may not like you any more than before, we were miserable or victorious together. The point is that I know how to work with you to get something done."

This experience can engender the opposite feeling, too. In that trying environment, people often discover traits in coworkers they find thoroughly revolting. They see negative behaviors or attitudes they did not associate with the person because they thought it was her job to be "like that." A supervisor who does not listen to other people at work would probably not listen to other people in the Leading Concepts training, either—regardless of whether he was a "private" or a "sergeant."

In Dean's field training, a participant's job could be to act as top leader during one mission, a team leader in the next, and a regular soldier in another. There is no correlation between a person's rank at work and his rank in the woods. Those shifts in role elicit some of the same mental agility, self-awareness, and different perspective as does the experiential training the Agency conducts.

Role-Playing

Before jumping out of a perfectly good airplane to do a formation skydive, the jumpers do a dirt dive. They go through all of the motions of leaving the plane, moving toward each other, taking hold of the adjacent skydiver's jumpsuit, and then moving to the next formation in an earthbound re-creation of the one-minute experience that will occur in the air. Dirt diving is the skydiver's version of role-playing—something you do to reprogram yourself with a conditioned response so that you do not revert to a natural one.

The Agency conducts many exercises that bring role-playing to the forefront in order to hone recruitment skills. As much as corporate people in training sessions may complain about it—"it's just acting"—role-playing is a valuable training tool that can prepare people mentally and even physically for real-life situations. For example, case officers go through extensive role-playing as part of their training—for essentially the same reason as skydivers dirt-dive. In both a recruitment drill and a skydive, the pressure is high and the urgency for "getting it right" cannot be ignored.

People in business have many of the same kinds of demands as Agency officers and skydivers, just to a different degree. And yet the mere suggestion that they should engage in role-playing often meets with resistance. It's a big bother, involving made-up dialogue. Yet role-playing is, in fact, a training device for excellence. It gives men and women substantial practice in applying the research they have done to prepare for a presentation or meeting. It is a tool for moderating the fear of rejection and mitigating the possibility of it.

Practicing Your Core Role The Agency's case officers adopt multiple roles when working the field, so they have to be actors. Businesspeople create distinct advantages for themselves when they cultivate the same ability and disadvantages when they stick to the same role all the time.

Some businesspeople hang on to the role of CEO or director of marketing when they're with their spouse and kids. It's also not appropriate to "mom" someone at work. If you behave the same way at work as you do when you're organizing a neighborhood clean-up, you have your roles mixed up. If you talk to your spouse the same way you talk to the head of the accounting department, you have your roles mixed up.

Because each role in the field must be distinct and consistent for a Clandestine officer, they approach the portrayal with the sophistication of a professional actor. They rehearse, and the rehearsals help them refine their story, mannerisms, dress, and other presentational elements. When I was overseas on an assignment, I periodically had to perform tasks that a foreign government might well consider unlawful acts. And yet, when I came back to the United States, I resumed my life as a law-abiding citizen. I had to be able to compartmentalize the behavior, to separate the roles, in order to act appropriately wherever I was.

Some people do not succeed in business past a certain level because they either don't grasp the importance of playing a role to match the context or they don't have the ability to do so. By not even trying, though, they wall themselves in professionally from the start. A senior executive should be wary about promoting someone to director on the basis of performance as manager if that person has never exhibited the behavior of director.

I had an Agency colleague called Don who came to me for counseling when I was part of the team running a day-long business simulation, in which all participants played roles in a fictional company. After receiving his feedback from his performance, he asked me about his own career. An engineer, he knew he was equal in knowledge to those senior to him, but he couldn't seem to break through, to get promoted to higher rank and responsibilities. I told him that the team observers had noticed that he had brought a lot of knowledge to the table throughout the day's exercise, but he hadn't behaved like the senior company officer he aspired to be in real life.

I suggested that he closely observe the behavior and actions of those in the ranks he aspired to join, and see if there weren't some behaviors that might be appropriate for him to adopt. In other words, you may not be a Senior Intelligence Service (SIS) executive, but you can act like one. I didn't see Don until many months later, at which time he walked up to me and said that what I said was the best career advice he had ever gotten. Whatever you aspire to be, act like one! And remember—the bottom line is that acting isn't everything; you still need the professional wherewithal to perform the job.

The world of business, as in the world of espionage, contains its share of bad actors. These people take two forms: those who have identified the role they need to play but can't carry it off, and those who have identified the role and "live it" in a prolonged, delusional episode. We have seen many people come to tragic ends because they assumed the role of Rambo, for example—copycats who found the wrong hero.

The actor who can't act is probably more common in both venues. These people know what they are supposed to do and how to behave, but they can't pull it off. An example we see all the time in Washington, D.C., is the former military officer who is hired by a company for sales, lobbying, and contract-management roles. The premise is that the person will be dealing with "his own," so he has an advantage. Well, he might have an advantage getting in the door, but once through the door and sitting at the meeting table, he likely reverts to military behavior instead of that of a professional who sells, persuades, and negotiates for a living.

There is help for these folks, and it's the same kind of help we give new Clandestine officers. It's the same kind of help that actors get after the great audition lands them the part in a new play. At the Agency, we called it role-playing. Actors call it rehearsal. In the world of business, it's often called simply coaching.

In the Agency, it was mandatory. In business, you're really lucky if you get it.

I think many corporations fail in helping people develop in their roles and in identifying and honing new behaviors, and thereby doom a lot of potentially high performers to lower level positions, where they can't contribute their best work. Here's why: The corporations value specialization. If it were just that, though, it wouldn't be so bad, but they value specialization the way an ant colony values specialization. If this situation keeps up, the typical member of a corporate society—like the typical member of an ant colony—will start to show genetic mutation that allows him to do only a particular job. This may sound exaggerated, but they are very similar models.

As a result of valuing that specialization so highly, companies are often willing to invest only in continued training that relates directly to the employee's job. You're an engineer who wants to learn about Web-based marketing? Sorry. You're an engineer, so you get to learn only more about engineering.

Using the Role to Score Role-playing is a central concept in professional development. It is not about pretending to be someone you're not—and that is a difference between the spy profession and the business world. In business, it's about practicing your presentation of self as CEO or sales director or receptionist, rather than rehearsing your cover.

There are two ways to use one's role to progress in business:

1. *Playing up*—that is, adopting the attributes associated with the position aspired to.

2. *Playing to win*—that is, coalescing research and interpersonal skills to succeed in a presentation or negotiation.

One of my colleagues once worked with a woman who came to her secretarial job right out of high school. Very bright, clearly capable of intellectually challenging work, this young woman dressed as if she were still in high school. She chewed gum, she said "Hey" to guests in the office as if they were school buddies. At the risk of insulting her, my colleague told her, "You will never get promoted if you don't dress and act like a person at the next level." That young woman hated her at the time, but she changed her appearance and her manners. And she got promoted—again and again. Twenty years later, the young woman is now a middle-aged woman with a senior position at a trade association.

A friend of mine who trains sales professionals puts the new hires through exercises that begin with jabbing them with an awareness of who, and what, a sales call is all about. He begins by briefing one of the participants who will play the role of the prospect. He instructs that person to go into the "meeting" with a lot of emotional baggage—spouse wants a divorce, teenager got suspended from school this week, reinjured his back playing tennis, and after a big argument with that spouse who wants a divorce, he's a little hung-over right now.

Almost invariably, the person playing the role of the sales professional concludes that the prospect "didn't like me." Instead of the meeting being focused on the prospect's very real needs and difficult circumstances, the salesperson interprets distraction as non-interest and makes it "all about me." I go into the dynamics of such a meeting in Chapter 10 on "The Path of Persuasion," but the salient point here is that role-playing can arouse a basic awareness of how to pay attention to another person—a person who represents either success or failure for you.

Other Mind Games

Role-playing is a type of mind game, with other types of mind games focused on other kinds of self-development training. I'm not free to say how the Agency engenders soft skills like a winning attitude or the ability to reduce the effects of stress, but it's obvious that having these soft skills offers distinct advantages in a high-pressure situation.

If you want to counter negativity that undermines performance, here are three habits that have to change, regardless of how:

1. *Making excuses before taking on a challenge.* This is like a runner saying, "My ankle is sore today" prior to a marathon. Who believes people who say things like that before they even start the race?

2. *Revisiting mistakes while in the midst of a meeting, presentation, or other demanding situation.* If it's the wrong work or not a good answer to the question, the employee should move on.

3. *Anticipating trouble during a challenging situation.* You spot a concerned look on your boss's face, or see that someone who knows ten times more than you do about the subject you're addressing just sat down in the audience. As soon as you've let that throw you, you've lost your audience.

In the course of the nine years he led a secret life supplying information to the United States, Polish Colonel Ryszard Kuklinski regularly participated in meetings with Polish and Soviet authorities and had to maintain composure and the appearance of loyalty. As Benjamin Weiser (2004) recounts in vivid detail in his book *A Secret Life*, Kuklinski may have been well practiced at this, but he still had doubt about whether he was in some outward fashion leaking emotions that would betray him. Every step of the way, he knew that torture and execution could be around the corner. As time went on, he asked his Agency handlers for a suicide pill and detailed emergency exit plans for him and his family in case they had to flee with little notice. This plan was called exfiltrating, or smuggling someone out of country "black," meaning covertly. But his fear of such an possibility did not overcome his dedication to doing everything he could—in this case risking his life to help bring about an end to the Soviet domination of Poland.

Kuklinski had myriad logical reasons to fear sudden discovery, as do people in far less extreme situations. For some people, having to make a presentation shakes them to the core. Others find walking into a room with strangers a terrifying proposition. Fears like this give rise to another fear—fear of failure.

The fear of failure does not diminish an employee's value. The recommendation here is to invest in your employees' complete professional development. Training to hone skills directly related to the position has tremendous value, and it should continue as skills in the field evolve. But to increase the measurable value of most employees to your operation, as well as bolster retention of those top performers who have the greatest influence on company performance, you need to coach and train them with your eye on what those persons can contribute to the mission, both today and tomorrow.

CONTINUING EDUCATION

The two major types of continuing education in the Agency involve exposure to what colleagues in different areas of the Intelligence Community do on a day-to-day basis, and cultivation of a deeper knowledge of one's own area of operations. These experiences add depth to an officer's analytical abilities, agility in contingency planning, creative problem solving, and other aspects of critical thinking that are stimulated and reinforced in purposeful training.

Cracking the Stovepipe

In the Agency, information is deliberately compartmentalized so people have access only to what they need to know. As a person becomes more senior in the organization, the need to know grows and so the "stovepiping" expands. At the Agency, we crack the stovepipe—or, in the jargon of many companies, "get people out of their silos"—with a program known as the Mid-Career Course. The timing is particularly critical because the people in it are at the middle-manager level and usually are viewed as executive-level material. This may be the first exposure they have to what people in other areas do on a daily basis.

This mid-career course is when people learn about what's going on in the rest of the organization and they expand their thinking about problem solving via exposure to other parts of the Intelligence Community—and even organizations in the private sector. Different people in the Agency offer different presentations about their specific areas and fellow class-mates also brief the group on their disciplines: one's own group usually also visits companies and corporations in the private sector to learn about their hiring, management, performance evaluation, and other practices that might be applicable to their work. Do Lockheed directors or Starbucks managers have some style of communicating or an administra-tive process that provides an elegant solution to a problem one also faces? This immersion in corporate operations is a designated part of career development, and one of the most beneficial types of education offered at the Agency.

During this course, every participant makes a presentation about her job. An operations officer, for example, will find out from someone in the technology area how he spends his day. An administrative executive will learn what happens in the field. I have heard people say, "That was the most valuable course I've taken." This is because in the Agency—and in many companies—people tend to work within their own stovepipe or silo. The course, therefore, offers a view of the broader picture.

How does this work in the private sector? Maryann worked for a lob-bying group in Washington for seven years. The head count ranged from thirty to thirty-six employees during that time, and even for an organiza-tion that small, it had three distinct "business units": lobbying, statistics, and standards. She had the unique position of coordinating communica-tions activities for all three—unique because she and her staff were the only ones outside of the three-person accounting/human resources department who interfaced with all three business units. They did not appreciate each other's problems and did not celebrate each other's suc-cesses. They shared potato salad at the mandatory company picnic, but even at company parties, they stood in separate areas. The corporate stovepipes had physical, functional, and psychological manifestations. Ultimately, the three areas grew more separate. Eventually, each paid "rent" to the mother company. Each had offices and cubicles separate from the others in the office—a functional advantage, but a reinforcing of the lack of interaction. Finally, it became obvious that they would probably break apart, and they did.

Cross-Experience, Not Cross-Training

As do a growing number of private-sector companies, the Agency crafts a career path for high-potential employees by providing them with a broad range of work experiences. Both the individual professional and the organization benefit substantially from this kind of cross-culture education. From the individual employee's perspective, cross-culture education:

* Is a critical part of broadening a person's personal portfolio.

* Is a source of motivation, in that the employee develops a heightened sense of the bigger picture and a firmer grasp of company progress or regression.

That bird's-eye view of the business characterizes the senior executive's outlook, which is what an organization is seeking to develop in its upwardly mobile employees.

From the organization's point of view, cross-culture education:

* Is a way to see which aspects of a job get someone energized and which fail to engage the individual.

* Can be a way to get the maximum out of both talented individuals and teams.

Among other effects, the organization may see increased efficiency in inter-department communications and heightened ability to coordinate within the organization to accomplish the organization's goals.

Financial institutions have traditionally used a cross-experience approach to career advancement. Employees may start with personal banking, move to consumer lending, then go to commercial lending, after that mortgages, and at some point, make it to the investment side of the house. After all of that exposure, employees are ready to take on top-level responsibilities, first as district managers and then as regional ones.

One of the relatively new criteria for promotion to senior ranks of the Agency is to have served in another element of the Intelligence Community. If a person has been in the CIA all of his career, perhaps he will be given an opportunity to do a stint in the FBI to broaden his perspective. This isn't just a familiarization visit to see what's on the other side of the fence; this kind of complementary substantive experience is considered a stepping-stone to the senior ranks of the Agency.

In fact, when the government category of Senior Executive Service (SES) was created (the Intelligence Community equivalent of which is the Senior Intelligence Service, or SIS), in theory an employee was able to go anywhere and function as a senior officer or manager—that's government-wide, not just the Agency. The whole idea was to find out what the cultural differences are and be able operate with respect for them, and not in conflict with them.

I had exposure to a global consumer-products company that tried this approach with some success, in an experiment related to one of its personal-care products. The organization brought a representative of manufacturing into the marketing team for a period of time; both got a much closer understanding of the other's operations. A practical outcome was having both of them talk about the product with more of a consumer focus.

Since the 1980s, the Agency has created bureaucratic entities known as "centers," such as the Counterterrorism Center, Counterintelligence Center, and Counterproliferation Center. And while the centers remain under Agency management, there are officers there from other agencies of the Intelligence Community. Their function is to bring their expertise, as well as knowledge of the who and what of their own organizations. So, when a field report about terrorist activities arrives at, say, the Counterterrorism Center, an FBI representative can discern the value of the report to the FBI and will know which FBI office to alert. Similarly, a National Security Agency (NSA) representative performs the same function for the NSA. In short, by co-locating officers from the different components of the Intelligence Community in the center, their presence greatly facilitates the identification and transmission of significant "pieces of intelligence" within the Intelligence Community. People are assigned to those centers to spy—and I mean that in a healthy sense—because they need to know how the host agency works; in the process, they also bring their expertise and knowledge of their organizational affiliation to the center.

A post-9/11 development that is somewhat analogous are the state and local fusion centers throughout the United States that consolidate information from the local police, maybe immigration authorities, an FBI office, and probably local authorities. Their mission comes out of a common concern about terrorist activities. The Department of Homeland Security has deployed intelligence officers to fusion centers in half the states in the country as part of the coordinated effort to support the flow of information and raise local awareness of security issues.

Going to School

Under Admiral Stansfield Turner (USN Ret.), who served as director of central intelligence from 1977 to early 1981, the concept of an academy or "senior seminar" for Agency senior officers, CIA University, was created. Before coming to the agency, Turner had served as head of the Naval War College in Newport, Rhode Island. When he arrived there, he was taken aback by the country-club atmosphere prevailing. Officers attending did a few papers, played a little golf, and enjoyed nice extended lunches. He felt strongly that the college was supposed to prepare officers for flag rank, like the Army War College in Carlisle, Pennsylvania. He felt there should be standards and a curriculum. The decision he faced was whether to increase the workload incrementally or virtually overnight as a *blitzkrieg*—the World War II term used by the German Panzer assault forces to describe a sudden and overwhelming attack. He chose blitzkrieg. Students had to put their putters away and start hitting the books and produce some real academic work.

When he came to the Agency, Turner felt that people at the Agency lacked the commonality of experience that the war colleges give to military officers. For example, there might be an engineer in the Office of Science & Technology and an operations officer in the Directorate of Operations, neither of whom had much sense of each other's challenges and contributions. The war colleges were designed to provide mid-level military officers with a demanding educational experience that would prepare them for higher responsibilities. Turner wanted to create an institution like that for intelligence professionals.

At that time, the DCI headed the Intelligence Community, but he made a decision to try such a course within the agency only. Some dozen or so officers were assigned to what was called the nine-month Senior Seminar when it was first designed and launched. They had assigned reading, visited corporations to see what they could learn, and had as guest lecturers leading experts in foreign affairs, academics, senior military officers, and other notables. This experiment ended after Turner's departure.

Years later, the Agency did develop advanced courses for operations officers and analysts and other personnel. Finally, under George Tenet, the Agency developed something akin to what Stansfield Turner had envisioned years before: CIA University, which included a center for training in clandestine operations and the Sherman Kent School for Intelligence Analysis.

With the later restructuring of the Intelligence Community following the recommendations of the 9/11 Commission, an executive order established the position of Director of National Intelligence (DNI) to oversee the Intelligence Community, thus disestablishing one of the roles exercised by the Director of Central Intelligence (DCI). The DCI as a title disappeared and the individual chosen to head the Agency was designated the director of the Central Intelligence Agency. Under the newly formed DNI, an institution similar to the military war colleges took form—a National Intelligence University. So the Intelligence Community is committed to continuing education at the senior officer level on a continuing basis, as do the military services.

Companies are not nearly as generous with their education benefits for mid-level executives as they used to be, and I can see why past experience would cause that response. The way many companies in the 1980s handled executive education often did not seem to give a very good return on the investment. The CIA certainly can't spare high-potential people for two years while they take a break from their daily work and go through advanced degree programs. The companies that did that at their expense, and sometimes as part of the compensation package, set themselves up for disappointment unless they had an attractive career path lined up for those employees returning with master's degrees. Instead, employees would come back to work armed with MBAs and turn around and leave soon after that—often for higher positions elsewhere, once other companies realized their enhanced professional qualifications.

Too many company executives felt the real prize for the employee was the degree itself. They failed to offer the level of challenge and growth that the person felt was merited after earning the college or graduate degree. A second reason for the failure is that the degree program took employees out of the flow of work. As the pace of many businesses quickened, they came back to a radically altered work environment. A product line could change considerably, as well as the competitive landscape, management practices, and even the corporate culture.

Though the old models of executive education may not have worked, that does not mean that replacing education with training is a beneficial swap. Focusing on specific job skills in lieu of critical thinking skills and broadened perspective on business issues can stabilize an executive's value to the company, but it may not increase it.

The Agency's emphasis on using mentoring as part of its continuing education program seems to be an approach that more and more companies are finding yields the kind of benefits that formal education can deliver. In the corporate setting, I've seen that a very effective version of mentoring occurs with in-house coaches. The CIA's model has been focused on pairing senior people with junior people doing the same job. For obvious reasons, we can't bring in professional coaches and plant them in the workforce the way a company does, although I do think this is a smart way to give employees exposure to ideas that support both personal and career development. It doesn't cost as much as an MBA, but it may be more valuable. For one thing, personal coaching may spark an executive's initiative to invest his own money and time in taking college or graduate-level courses.

I find that many mid-level people miss, or misunderstand, some of the greatest opportunities for education that their companies frequently offer. For example, people in sales and marketing get sent to conferences and trade shows, which can serve as venues for education as long as the people attending them exploit the chances to learn. Probably one of the most underrated and misunderstood sessions is a presentation by a motivational speaker.

Your body of professional knowledge and skill is like gunpowder, and a good motivational speaker gives you the spark to light the gunpowder.

TWIN NECESSITIES: CONTINUING TRAINING AND EDUCATION

Keep the neurons firing in the heads of all of your officers and have a program to avoid the "hype cycle":

- Give employees mentoring from the beginning. Even if the right people are unavailable the first few days, make sure someone has the responsibility and resources to help the person feel connected to the mission. The process of engagement, or disengagement, starts immediately.

- Refine, retell, and institutionalize the stories that express how to make particular contributions, as well as why individuals are important to the organization.

- Appreciate the transferable skills that experiential learning cultivates; this is a type of training that deserves an untouchable line in the budget.

- A clear understanding of one's role in a given situation provides a definite competitive advantage. Role-playing upgrades important interpersonal skills.

- Negative habits lead to negative outcomes. Train people to recognize and get rid of these habits.

- When responsibilities of an officer involve a need to know how colleagues in different areas operate, crack the stovepipe in a formal way. Don't let the discoveries be ad hoc and unplanned.

- Athletes cross-train to improve performance; executives cross-experience. Knowing how to do someone else's job may not help you directly, but it may give you new insights and "aha!" moments to enhance your whole approach to your work.

- Study history. Study theories. Study heroes. Read professional books and journals. Take advantage of the rich material that is available today in many forms of media, including webinars and some social networks that help prepare you for your next advancement on your career path.

"To convert the hesitant businessman or fearful alien into a cooperative Source, the contact officer must have a wide variety of skills. He must be a salesman, selling his prospect on the importance of the intelligence function; he must be an intelligence officer, knowing the needs and the gaps in the community's information; he must play the practical psychologist, handling dissimilar personalities with dexterity; and finally, he becomes a skilled reporter, putting the Source's information into a concise and readable intelligence report."

—**Anthony F. Czajkowski,** "Techniques of Domestic Intelligence Collection," *Studies in Intelligence* 3, no. 1; Winter 1959; originally classified "Confidential."

The Intelligence Cycle

The Agency's intelligence cycle corresponds to the strategic planning cycle of a company. After a set of requirements is developed, the effort begins with the collection of information—the raw material of intelligence—and that involves exploiting the various collection mechanisms. The four major sources of intelligence collection are human intelligence (HUMINT), or running clandestine operations to recruit agents who can report timely, accurate, and objective information not available by other means; signals intelligence (SIGINT), which is information gathered through electronic and other signals intercepts; imaging intelligence (IMINT), or photos derived from reconnaissance satellites; and information available through open sources (OSINT). It isn't much different in business, except that the collection operations in business cannot usually be described as covert.

The next step in both environments is analysis, which is guided by key questions such as, "What portion of the information responds directly to the needs stated in the requirements?" "What can we verify as reliable?" and "Does the information reflect both logic and keen intuition?" And then, just as your company produces a product and/or service of value to your customers, the Agency produces intelligence in the form of reports to our main customers—the president of the United States and selected policymakers. Intelligence is, therefore, the primary output of the Agency and other organizations within the Intelligence Community. Having accomplished that delivery of product, we repeat the cycle. The decisions and judgments of our customers shape the new requirements, so we go back and collect new information and retool in areas that reflect an evolved mission.

The chapters in this section have titles that reflect the strategic process of the Agency, but the discussions focus on the parallels with businesses. As stated, the fundamental steps are: (1) we generate our output like most other companies, with accuracy, timeliness, and objectivity guiding the stages of moving the product to customers; and (2) once we have accomplished that mission, we start the intelligence cycle all over again.

Those stages, as shown in Figure 2-1, are:

1. Collection

2. Analysis

3. Dissemination

WHAT IS INTELLIGENCE?

The hallmark of an intelligence agency is to provide accurate, timely, and objective information to policymakers—that is the meaning of speaking truth to power, the primary role of the Intelligence Community. *How* those of us in operations acquire that information is what you mostly know about our work. For a moment, let's focus on the product of those covert collection operations rather than the mechanics of them.

When an industry analyst provides a company with business intelligence, theoretically that analyst is giving accurate, objective, and timely information that should help shape the organization's decisions. Not will, but *should*, because if it is intelligence in the same sense as the Agency uses the term, the information conveys meaning rather than just statistics and

Figure 2-1 The intelligence cycle.

The Agency	Company XYZ	
Collection of information on other countries and transnational issues from assets, use of technology, news reports, and so on, as well as running operations	Collection of market information from human sources such as customers, prospects, observation at trade shows, press releases, etc.	Raw material
Analysis of information to give the customer (President of the United States) what is most useful, something that supports sound decision making	Assessment of information with an eye on producing the product or service that gives the company an edge and addresses customers' needs	Processing assembly
Dissemination to the President and other key policymakers	Launch of product or service	Mission accomplished

raw facts. There is an added value in connecting the dots and knowing which dots are just specks on the page.

In addition to being meaningful, a critical element of Agency intelligence is that it is secret. It is acquired by any one of the collection mechanisms and then processed and forwarded to the analysts, who have access to all forms of collection including material from open sources, or OSINT. Case officers collect information that is not collectable by other means, such as on the Internet or in foreign news broadcasts, and that secret information is often sent to the Agency analysts in its raw form, where it may be used as a "stand-alone" item of intelligence or be combined with material from other collection mechanisms.

Information that qualifies as business intelligence should meet the same standards of being inaccessible by open-source means and exclusively prepared for a customer. If an industry analyst sells the organization "business intelligence" for $5,000, and a competitor can buy it for the same $5,000, then it's "business insights" or "business information," but not "business intelligence." Any credible assertion that the Agency did not meet all three criteria of accurate, timely, and objective translates to "You failed in your mission to deliver the product you were assigned to deliver."

CHAPTER **FIVE**

Collection—
Challenges and Techniques

The CIA exists because of the U.S. government's need for information relating to any real or perceived threats to the nation's national security. The business activities of the Agency are collection, analysis, and reporting. It sounds sexier to emphasize efforts to thwart terrorist attacks and influence events abroad, such as national elections, but those are covert actions that may follow from good intelligence reporting and are undertaken only with presidential direction and coordination within the executive branch.

THE CHALLENGE OF INFORMATION COLLECTION

As the chart at the beginning of Section 2 shows, regardless of the product the Agency or business organization ends up delivering to its customers, we both start with a need for information. And that means we have common challenges in collecting it.

In defining your company's information requirements, consider some words of wisdom from former Secretary of Defense Donald Rumsfeld, who delivered the following on "The Unknown" at a February 12, 2002, Department of Defense news briefing. At the time, pundits ridiculed the poetic flight, but the substance withstands scrutiny.

> As we know, there are known knowns. There are things we know we know. We also know there are known unknowns. That is to say we know there are some things we do not know. But there are also unknown unknowns, the ones we don't know we don't know.

A known known would be how many companies manufacture a product that competes with yours. A known unknown might be where those competing products are currently installed. An unknown unknown could be some aspect of the service agreement that is the only incentive a customer might have to purchase your main competitor's product instead of yours.

In the first category, you don't need a cadre of information collectors to secure the facts. You can open a trade publication and find that out or you can do a quick Google search. The second category, however, requires some research. Depending on the product, a known unknown may range from simple to very complicated research. The unknown unknowns, however, are answers to questions that you don't even know you should be asking. That information can surface accidentally, or it can surface as a result of ongoing collection efforts and will feed into ongoing analytical efforts that are systematically reported to decision makers.

Our relationship with Polish Colonel Ryszard Kuklinski proved enormously valuable in discovering the "unknown unknowns" about Soviet intentions and plans from the early 1970s to the early 1980s (also see Chapter 4). One example was Ryszard's description of supposed military exercises involving 44,000 Polish troops who were actually part of a Soviet design to quash the Solidarity movement through martial law. On March 5, 1981, Langley cabled officers in Warsaw that Ryszard's information was so critical to interpreting future events—and exposure would have such grave consequences for him—that the Agency restricted it to the president of the United States, vice president, and the secretaries of state and defense. It was just what the Reagan administration needed to take appropriate action. A public statement indicating that the world was keeping an eye on the "exercises" put the spotlight on what the Soviets called Soyuz 81. It was, in effect, a PR blockade.

Consider now a hypothetical scenario of intelligence gathering related to al-Qaeda to illustrate how this might work today. The president and his policymakers would like to learn of al-Qaeda's plans and capabilities. Since we've been tasked to find out that information, we create operations to that end, though the chances we will succeed are mixed. Nevertheless, we may develop intelligence related to that subject that gives us insight into the larger picture. For example, we may find out about a group in Indonesia forming a terrorist unit on behalf of al-Qaeda—information that has not been known until now. We have come upon something brand-new that is of interest, even though no one has asked us about it. It is an unknown unknown, since we were not specifically looking for information about al-Qaeda in Indonesia, but our worldwide collections efforts resulted in our acquiring some useful facts.

It's highly significant and adds to the developing overall picture of al-Qaeda, and of its plans and capabilities, even though no one has asked for that specifically. So the Agency is both responding to tasking and responding to the spirit of the mission, as well as to the letter of the job at hand. The responder is like a trip wire—a small military unit that serves as an early alert system, the first line of tactical intelligence in combat operations.

There are many corporate examples of when unknown unknowns took over and, in a practical sense, determined the fate of a product. The Segway is an example of a concept defeated by the unknown unknowns. Heralded at its debut as the solution to short-distance travel, this two-wheeled personal mobility vehicle had a promising future. But a high price point and regulatory snafus in different jurisdictions, combined with sociological factors regarding its acceptance, kept a lot of question marks alive when the product hit the market.

The reusable adhesive that enabled the birth of the Post-it note was an R&D failure. Among the unknown unknowns were that Art Fry, a colleague of the original inventor Spencer Silver, would take action on the low-stick adhesive five years later and millions of people would agree with Fry that it could be used in all manner of ways.

* * *

If you uncover information that may have a bearing on the "unknown unknowns" and have nowhere to go with it, then what good is it? This is precisely the quandary that many companies create for themselves. Sometimes companies don't know what they, in fact, already know but have failed to integrate. That is why having some form of intelligence unit can serve as valuable a function as any other core department, like marketing or accounting. You want people to have the job of collecting and analyzing the body of available information, systematically.

Let's say your company has construction contracts that require an extended presence somewhere. It doesn't matter whether those contracts are in Amman, Jordan, or in Biloxi, Mississippi; everyone who goes there—sales, marketing, senior executives, engineers, laborers—is your antenna (your collector of information). Each will learn things that can help the company competitively. If you can get them to report what they learn systematically to a central intelligence unit, the company is in a stronger position to get other contracts in that same location, as well as elsewhere. You will find you knew more than you thought you knew. Those people in the intelligence unit—and there may be only one or two—also spend their time reading *BusinessWeek* and the *Wall Street Journal*, as well as checking out blogs and watching TV news shows.

We can also do a variation on Rumsfeld's insight levels that approaches the topic from a different angle. It is another way of suggesting how to secure competitive intelligence systematically:

- There are people who know what you need to know—your primary information sources.

- There are people who can identify others who have the knowledge you are seeking—your secondary sources.

For example, suppose you have reason to believe that your main competitor will release a new product, but you don't know when. If you did know when, you might be able to make a preemptive strike through a new marketing campaign, timing your customer visits differently, and meeting ahead with prospects. The one person who knows for sure when this new product will appear is the CEO of the company. She is the one who knows. You have no way of getting to her, so your best bet is to find someone who has direct and regular access to her, because that is a person who might also have the information you need. And so you begin your search by reading company materials and the media coverage to ascertain who those people are who are within your reach—who are in the inner circle of the CEO.

There is, of course, the information that you can't possibly know unless you're a mind reader. Sometimes this situation does apply to business information, because the CEO of a company may hold a particular decision so close to his chest that few others have a clue about it until he issues a decree to do this or go there.

For instance, Saddam Hussein amassed his troops at the gates of Kuwait, but the intelligence question remained: Would he invade? Regardless of having the tanks and people ready, and understanding what he had to gain and lose, the decision rested solely with Saddam Hussein, and he could do as he had done many times before—change his mind at the last minute. Even having his right-hand man in your pocket at the moment would not have made a difference if Saddam himself had not yet made his decision.

In short, even with the best information in the world, you may not know what the outcome will be. On the question of weapons of mass destruction, Saddam Hussein led his own generals and commanders to believe that he was pursuing the development of such weapons. He was deceiving his own people. So even if we had communication with sources close to him, we would have gotten a false reading.

Think of the debacles at Enron and on Wall Street, if you think that doesn't happen in business. Many people close to the ultimate source—a manipulator and con man like Bernard Madoff, for example—think things are one way when they are really going another way.

A contributing factor to this misinformation is stovepiping, or confining the information within silos. The business executive gets to know the information in his stovepipe, and what he knows is strictly controlled by those who work within that stovepipe. If he isn't connected to other sources of information, receiving any cross-flow, he can find himself doing bogus accounting or inflating a product's benefits to customers without even realizing that he is lying.

* * *

At what point do you decide that the intelligence you have is "actionable"—that is, you have *sufficient* intelligence to take some action? The process of creating the most ideal scenario, given the limitations, involves the following:

- Looking at past behavior and trying to find patterns and strong indicators.

- Keeping an eye on the people closest to the primary source or the decision-making group, who may tip their hands one way or another about what they know.

- Going after peripheral information that could point toward the information you really need.

In the case of gathering information on Saddam and the troops at the Kuwaiti border, it would have been useful if someone in the field reported an Iraqi purchase of 500 laminated cards containing Kuwaiti slang phrases. That might mean nothing more than Saddam's trying to deceive people with a distraction, but it is one more bit of data to throw in the information mix being analyzed with an idea toward taking action.

TARGETED SOURCES

When you think about your own information sources to gain a competitive advantage in business, the targeted ones involving human intelligence (HUMINT) are customers, prospects, competitors, and consultants. But the world of espionage may teach you how you can get that information.

I was on a shuttle bus recently, going from an airport parking lot to the terminal. A female executive across the aisle answered her cell phone early in the ride and proceeded to tell the caller why she had hired a particular consultant, why she didn't hire someone else, exactly what she was paying the person to do, and what that person's success would mean to her biotech firm. She was probably safe in doing that because the chances of a competitor's being on that bus were pretty slim.

She would not be quite so safe on the shuttle bus to the airport from a hotel that had housed an industry conference, however, or in the airport lounge just after a trade show has wrapped up. She also would not be safe at a restaurant or bar anywhere near an industry event. In those locations, overhearing something of value need not be a random event. You can plan it.

Since you're not the chatty airhead on the cell phone, but you are the good listener who would never do that, take advantage of those who do chat openly, and often loudly, on their cell phones and in conversations; they paid no attention the day they got the briefing on protecting company information. Here are some tips on casual eavesdropping for when you're in the vicinity of talkative and inattentive competitors:

* When you spot a competitor, get in back of him at the cab stand and find out what hotel he's going to. Chances are his colleagues are staying there as well. Go to that hotel bar and listen to conversations; some of the competitor's reps might even still have their name badges or polo shirts on, so you don't even have to sniff around to find them.

* If you want to find out where your competitors are staying and don't want to hang out at the cab stand, then call the hotels in the area and find out where those competitors have corporate rates. Some companies even post this information on their Web sites. Go have breakfast at those hotels and listen to how your competitors are planning to spend their day.

* Pay the fee to get you into an airport lounge before your flight back home after a trade show. Show up at the airport four hours early, go to the lounge, and listen to the cell phone calls and chats at the "free" bar.

• If you're a woman, listen to the conversation in the bathroom at the convention center. (Men generally don't chat in that venue, but women do—or so I'm told.)

Your thoroughness in using technology to assist you in getting information can also reflect a spylike approach to collection. In the world of espionage, you would recognize only two ways of getting information— through open-source means and the many covert collection systems. But there might be a more nuanced way of characterizing sources of information for business: open-source, proprietary information that can be purchased, and information accessible only by covert means.

Companies have plenty of access to the first two, but rarely take advantage of everything else that is available. The basics include competitors' press releases, news coverage of their activities, updates to Web sites that would include new marketing material, and speeches given by their senior executives. Tracking them on the Internet is fairly easy with Google searches. Among the openly accessible proprietary or private information you can readily acquire are such items as profiles in *Hoover's* database and reports from industry analysts.

Does anyone on your staff track the social networking sites, as well as the professional networking sites? As of this writing, there are about 150 such networking sites that give some indication of who knows what and what their interests are. I did a random search on LinkedIn.com to test the system. I just wanted to find one person who was accessible to me who had some connection to a high-profile businessman I'd met once at an event. I found not one but six people with whom I had some sort of connection who were also connected to this individual. You might also want to get your competitors' and prospective customers' blogs and tweets. You can find out about someone's neighborhood—or even an individual house— just by checking Google Earth. Sure, utilizing all these sources will yield an enormous amount of information—perhaps too much—to make a difference to your operations. If you have a clear agenda and know why the information might have value, then you have established a requirement for it. Once you have that requirement, the collection and analysis should become important and ongoing elements of your business activities.

When a number of field officers and analysts left the CIA after the dissolution of the Soviet Union in 1991, some of them approached companies in the private sector to encourage them to build an intelligence component into their companies. The aim was to teach them how to collect and collate information from all sources that would give them an edge over a competitor. They were not trying to teach companies how to conduct espionage, but simply how to be more systematic and analytical in collecting and processing information.

They wanted to introduce the practical ramifications of rooting their business decisions in intelligence and in what are known as intelligence estimates, which are basically excellent extrapolations. In his book, *Inside the CIA*, Ron Kessler (1992) makes this point very effectively, in pointing to what a Presidential Daily Brief (PDB, a small newspaper-like report of intelligence highlights prepared by Agency analysts every morning for the president) might have looked like just days before the Pearl Harbor bombings—if only there had been an organization of "central intelligence" at the time.

In creating a mock briefing, Kessler cites what people like Harold P. Ford, formerly with the CIA's National Intelligence Council, documented about what facts were known three days before the attack. Ford wrote an entire book devoted to the importance of estimative intelligence that was published by the Defense Intelligence College. These intelligence estimates, the product of keen analysis of the raw information available from HUMINT, SIGINT, and other sources, would have resulted in something that looked like this:

For the past two weeks, Japan has been warning its diplomats that war may be imminent . . . there have been these other signs that Japan may be preparing to go to war:

* On Nov. 22, Foreign Minister Togo informed Ambassador Nomura that negotiations between Japan and the United States must be settled by November 29 because after that "things are going automatically to happen."

- For the past two weeks, the Japanese have been padding their radio messages with garbled or old messages to make decoding more difficult.

- Three days ago, the Japanese Imperial Navy changed its ship call signs. This is an unprecedented change, since they had just been changed. Normally they are switched every six months.

- Two days ago, the Japanese Foreign Ministry ordered its consulates in six cities—including Washington—to destroy all but the most important codes, ciphers, and classified material.

- Three days ago, the U.S. became unable to locate previously tracked Japanese submarines.

- Scattered, unconfirmed reports indicate naval air units in southern Japan have been practicing simulated torpedo attacks against ships there.

This wasn't the only evidence by a long shot if you combine it with the personal reports of soldiers like William Sanchez on Corregidor in the Philippines, who reported to his commander that he saw Japanese vessels moving toward Hawaii. The point is, you can have all the facts you need to establish a competitive advantage, but if you do not have a mechanism for processing them and relating them to one another, and for delivering the intelligence to the key decision maker, then the information is worthless. This is the nub of making maximum use of all the information you have collected or have access to: connecting the dots. History will appreciate its value, but you won't benefit from it one bit.

ALTERNATE SOURCES

One of my later assignments with the Agency was serving as chief of the executive development staff. I made various efforts to bring in speakers and experiences from outside the Agency. I brought in guest speakers whom I thought would be interesting and provocative. Different kinds of speakers participated in this program. At one point, I brought in Theodore Draper, who wrote *Very Thin Line* about the Iran-Contra affairs. He was highly critical of the Agency's role in Iran-Contra; I felt it was important for our senior officers to hear dissenting views.

I also brought in Dr. David Charney, a psychiatrist who had refined his views about how to keep people from becoming traitors to the point of developing a counterintelligence program he was trying to interest Agency and FBI counterintelligence offices in. An expert on the psychology of spies, he had developed professional insights into Earl Pitts, the FBI Special Agent who turned into a KGB spy; Robert Hanssen, the notorious FBI Special Agent who also became a KGB spy; and Brian Regan, of the U.S. Air Force and National Reconnaissance Office. David is still active in consulting and promoting his program. His premise is that the government should establish an office that can be contacted by government employees who have started down the path of betraying their country, perhaps impulsively, but who would like to "reverse course." He believes that providing such a safety valve would serve to prevent some would-be traitors from doing their worst. As it is, he believes, once embarked down the path of betrayal, individuals find there is no way to turn back and so they end up doing the maximum amount of damage.

And then, quite by accident, there was Norman Mailer. He had done a book called *Harlot's Ghost*, a novel published in 1992 that *Publishers Weekly* described as "a mammoth imagining of the CIA that puts all previous fictions about the Agency in the shade." I was in the now-defunct Crown Books in McLean, Virginia, and at a little table sat Norman Mailer, signing books. I made the decision on the spot to ask him to speak at the Agency. I stood in line with the others waiting for him to sign their copies of *Harlot's Ghost*, and when it was my turn, I handed him my card and said, "When you have a couple of minutes, I'd like to speak with you." He looked at the card with the CIA seal and immediately said, "Sure."

When he had a break in the book signing, he found me two aisles away in the store. I asked him if he would like to speak to a CIA audience, and he agreed to do it. He didn't have any cards with him, so I pulled out my wallet to get my cards so he could write his contact information on the back of one of them. He wrote down his name and number and handed me the card. After browsing in the store some more, I decided to buy a book, but when I went to pay for it, I realized my wallet was gone. I got back in line at the table where Mailer had resumed his signing. When I got to the front, I said, "Norman, I believe you have my wallet." He reached into his pocket and pulled out two wallets—his and mine! He autographed my copy of *Harlot's Ghost* with the words, "To Peter. We'll remember how we met." And I'll never forget the broad grin and twinkle in his eye.

When he came to speak to our group, Mailer talked about research he did for *Harlot's Ghost*. He asserted that he could tell the Soviet Union was falling apart before we did because the hotel soap smelled bad and there was not enough toilet paper. As cavalier as they sound, those are potentially relevant observations from a well-traveled, bright individual that you would be unwise to dismiss as simply glib remarks.

The Agency already knew these things, but the point is that you never know where you will find nuggets of information. Norman Mailer had an instinct for doing what every good case officer does—and records in contact reports, rather than novels. He knew two interrelated things that business professionals should keep in mind as they enter new environments inhabited by competitors and prospects. First, nobody in the world is unimportant; you don't network only with the people you think are important, but with everyone who has a role in the grand scheme. Second, you look for both the positives and the negatives, evidence of both success and decay.

NO STONE UNTURNED

All of the information collected from a broad array of sources through multiple means might be put into the bucket called "research, "or "raw material," as suggested by the earlier chart. You cannot have too much research as long as it is germane to the mission; it may not be immediately useful, but it could well fit into the puzzle at a later time.

In the business environment, Bridgewater Associates has been reported by the financial media and analysts as a great success story that illustrates the high value of exhaustive research. Working out of a spare room in his house in 1975, founder Ray Dalio built an investment firm managing about $80 billion. His impressive, consistent returns seem to be the result of relentless searching by his human and computer resources for investment opportunities. He sounds like Goldilocks: he doesn't want it too hot, or too cold; he wants it just right. And he seems to find it. His Pure Alpha hedge fund leads the list of the world's most successful, topping J.P. Morgan Chase, Paulson & Co., and all the others.

The lesson here is that you could have the best analysts in the world working for you, but unless they have a sufficient amount of good, raw material to analyze, the result will be a set of educated guesses. (Hold on to your objections.) Although they used different phrases to say the same thing, the Bush administration's defense of pre-9/11 actions, or nonactions, after receiving the following briefing came down to the fact that the PDB contained "background information" and speculation—but not actionable intelligence on al-Qaeda's plans to attack. As a reminder, "intelligence" is validated information put into a useful context. But as I explore further in the upcoming chapter on analysis, in some cases intelligence actually is educated guesses because the right people are doing the analysis.

In business, keen minds can see something as fragmented and speculative as the brief shown below and are able to predict the actions of a competitor. This is the kind of mind, in fact, that industry research firms, trade media, and companies seek.

Bin Ladin Determined to Strike in US

Clandestine, foreign government, and media reports indicate Bin Ladin since 1997 has wanted to conduct terrorist attacks in the U.S. Bin Ladin implied in U.S. television interviews in 1997 and 1998 that his followers would follow the example of World Trade Center bomber Ramzi Yousef and "bring the fighting to America."

After U.S. missile strikes on his base in Afghanistan in 1998, Bin Ladin told followers he wanted to retaliate in Washington, according to a (phrase redacted) service.

An Egyptian Islamic Jihad (EIJ) operative told an (phrase redacted) service at the same time that Bin Ladin was planning to exploit the operative's access to the U.S. to mount a terrorist strike.

The millennium plotting in Canada in 1999 may have been part of Bin Ladin's first serious attempt to implement a terrorist strike in the U.S. Convicted plotter Ahmed Ressam has told the FBI that he conceived the idea to attack Los Angeles International Airport himself, but that Bin Ladin lieutenant Abu Zubaydah encouraged him and helped facilitate the operation. Ressam also said that in 1998 Abu Zubaydah was planning his own U.S. attack.

Ressam says Bin Ladin was aware of the Los Angeles operation.

Although Bin Ladin has not succeeded, his attacks against the U.S. Embassies in Kenya and Tanzania in 1998 demonstrate that he prepares operations years in advance and is not deterred by setbacks. Bin Ladin associates surveilled our Embassies in Nairobi and Dar es Salaam as early as 1993, and some members of the Nairobi cell planning the bombings were arrested and deported in 1997.

Al-Qa'ida members—including some who are U.S. citizens—have resided in or traveled to the U.S. for years, and the group apparently maintains a support structure that could aid attacks. Two al-Qa'ida members found guilty in the conspiracy to bomb our Embassies in East Africa were U.S. citizens, and a senior EIJ member lived in California in the mid-1990s.

A clandestine source said in 1998 that a Bin Ladin cell in New York was recruiting Muslim-American youth for attacks.

We have not been able to corroborate some of the more sensational threat reporting, such as that from a (phrase redacted) service in 1998 saying that Bin Ladin wanted to hijack a U.S. aircraft to gain the release of "Blind Shaykh" 'Umar' Abd al-Rahman and other U.S.-held extremists.

Nevertheless, FBI information since that time indicates patterns of suspicious activity in this country consistent with preparations for hijackings or other types of attacks, including recent surveillance of federal buildings in New York.

The FBI is conducting approximately 70 full field investigations throughout the U.S. that it considers Bin Ladin-related. CIA and the FBI are investigating a call to our Embassy in the UAE in May saying that a group of Bin Ladin supporters was in the U.S. planning attacks with explosives.

For the President Only

6 August 2001

Declassified and Approved for Release, 10 April 2004

TECHNIQUES OF COLLECTION

This book would have been very easy to write if the Agency had the magic powers that some people ascribe to it—the tactical advantages that belong only to comic-book superheroes. All I would have to do is divulge the formula for the magic, and voilà! You would make more money.

The fact is that a lot of the tactical success in the intelligence business has its roots in the judgment, intellect, skills, and instincts of individual officers. From time to time, that wisdom gets codified in a way that provides guidance for others in the field in their collection efforts and provides nuggets of practical guidance for people in other lines of work.

Following are some typical Agency techniques for collecting information that could well apply to business, as well.

The Moscow Rules

A classic example is what became known as the Moscow Rules, a rough list of what might be called street tips that were developed over time in Moscow Station. They were operating techniques learned the hard way by case officers who were working the Moscow streets in the face of nearly round-the-clock surveillance by local intelligence and law enforcement. Here is a sampling of the tips that show how bits and pieces of information learned on the street and through close observance can be collated and made into useful guidelines for others. Tony Mendez, a former senior CIA officer in technical operations support and an Advisory Board member at the International Spy Museum, recorded them:

- Assume nothing.

- Never go against your gut.

- Establish a distinctive and dynamic profile and pattern.

- Stay consistent over time.

- Be nonthreatening; keep them relaxed; mesmerize!

- Know the opposition and their terrain intimately.

- Make sure you can anticipate your destination.

- Don't harass the opposition.

- Keep your options open.

- Once is an accident; twice is a coincidence; three times is an enemy action.

- Pick the time and the place for action.

- There is no limit to a human being's ability to rationalize the truth.

Many professions and many industries have their own versions of the Moscow Rules. One public relations and marketing agency serving high-tech companies established the following, which might better be called "Silicon Valley Rules" because of the company's location and focus:

- Ask questions to clarify.

- Develop a daily task list of realistic deadlines.

- Plan ahead with a prioritized to-do list.

- Know your personal limits and ask for help when necessary.

- Set client expectations.

- Know when to let go; collaborate and trust your coworkers.

- Work for team consensus.

- Anticipate what could go wrong.

- Be specific in instructions.

- Know when to shut out the world; and respect others' quiet time.

- Set an agenda and stick to it.

- Establish roles for meetings.

- Stick to your goals; adjust as needed.

Reading In—Beyond Google

When comedian Stephen Colbert came to the International Spy Museum to tape an interview with me for his TV show, *The Colbert Report,* he had already told viewers that the economic crisis had necessitated looking for a "fallback position." He thought that "spy" might be the career he would adopt just in case he lost his job. Walking into my office, he knew more about me than some people who see me at work every day. He had *read in.* And his producers had collected no end of useful information about me and the Museum.

When we assign someone to a new overseas station, the person may have limited experience with the day-to-day workings in that environment. In addition to talking with people at Headquarters who have served there, we have them "read in"—that is, they read the back files on our operations and activities in that country. The officials in that country have watched us come and go over a period of decades; they have us down cold—our personalities, our habits, our successes, and especially our failures. The new officer has to background himself as much as possible about our record in that country and our current relationships.

Fortunate Accidents

In the world of espionage, there are often "planned" accidents for operational purposes. In one case, we wanted to dangle someone in front of a Soviet agent to see if they would try to recruit him. That is, we wanted to plant someone squarely in front of a Soviet intelligence officer, so we observed him. What time did he come home from work? What time did he turn the lights off at night?

We then got a car and rigged it to fail. We had this individual drive the car and trigger a failure in a spot where he and the Soviet would be alone. The meeting seemed completely accidental. The Soviet got out and helped him—as we expected. He found him of interest—as we expected. The relationship grew from there.

Does this sound like anything to you? Business? Maybe not. It's actually more like dating. A guy "accidentally" manages to sit next to a woman he has his eyes on; reverse the genders and the same thing is equally true. Suddenly, two people are having coffee and the whole thing seems incredibly fortuitous. The chance meeting that can lead to a lifetime of happiness. Or at least a few months of it.

Cultural Sensitivity

A nation can have a culture. A neighborhood can have a culture. Clubs, religious groups, schools, and companies all have individual cultures. Each family has its own culture. In trying to forge connections with a new prospect, you need to take into account the various "cultures" that have formed the environment for your prospect. Adjust your communication to the culture that affects how she's thinking and behaving at the moment.

When I talk about the essence of field operations being that of recruiting, and that the way that officers recruit is that they get to know people and develop relationships, keep in mind that we are developing those relationships in different cultures. We are cultivating trust with people in a different country and different culture and, in many cases, in another language. Those are extraordinary challenges.

Business is short of people who can meet those challenges in different countries over time, but companies usually don't see the need to develop them, either. If a company wants to do business in Japan, it might hire Japanese people. The CIA doesn't have that luxury; the Agency can only hire American citizens. We may recruit Japanese men and women as agents, but we can't employ them as staff members. Companies, however, need to consider the strategic advantages of giving loyal employees the training that will enable them to go to foreign countries and work effectively. The company becomes more human to them; the connection to the mission becomes more personal.

Not long after completing the assignment to head up the Shevchenko task force, Fred Hitz, then the Agency's legislative counsel, asked me to join the Office of Legislative Affairs. He wanted operations officers to conduct liaison with the Hill so that the senators, representatives, and their staffs would appreciate that they were dealing with senior operations officers with field experience. He asked me to head up the unit dealing with the Senate. I had little experience dealing with the Hill when I accepted the position. As a CIA operations officer, I was used to dealing with other cultures; Congress was one more "foreign" culture. Six years later, when I became the chief of the Agency's executive development staff, I designed a familiarization course called "Briefing Congress." I created an ad hoc panel of four or five people to serve as our "members of Congress," and then I briefed them on how to behave during hearings at which the students appeared. It was up to the students, then, to adapt to the congressional "behavior."

"Reading" a culture is intimately related to speaking a foreign language and reading body language. It starts with a sensitivity that differences exist, and then builds on close observation and experience with the people with whom you need to connect.

Situational Awareness

Situational awareness relates to people, situations, and information. I heard a story recently about renowned economist Mark Zandi. He got into a cab and, after shutting the door, asked the cab driver, "How's business?" It wasn't an idle question to initiate chit-chat with the driver. Learning the answer to this question enhances his situational awareness about the economy—and that's what people count on him to have.

Athletes often talk about situational awareness as a highly tuned perception they develop after performing over and over in a variety of settings and atmospheres. It reflects the development of acute sensory capabilities so that reaction time compresses, ability to anticipate improves, and the person remembers and describes a lot more of what went on. On a first skydive, for example, a person's situational awareness probably isn't all that good. The individual is on sensory overload, so he could be looking straight down at the ground and not absorb any details—like the fact that he was falling toward a lake. All of that changes with more and more skydives.

Expand that concept of situational awareness and you start to see how many other factors affect your ability to function at the highest level possible in a high-pressure environment. Maybe you're an experienced jumper, but find that you cannot be fully aware of what's happening during the skydive—you're distracted—unless you have done a complete gear check, double-tied your shoelaces, and are wearing your favorite black gloves. The alert person learns over time what factors must come together so she can be at the top of her game. A person with inconsistent situational awareness has never bothered to examine what factors are present when she performs extremely well.

After I left the Agency, one of my pursuits in the private sector was to coach managers and executives on their presentation skills. Early on, I would tell people to go into the room where they will be presenting. They should know how the room is set up, whether any distractions need to be removed, where the light switch is so it can be flicked quickly to "go to black," what the temperature is—all of that is situational awareness.

I had a colleague who retired from the government at the age of fifty-four after thirty years' service, and she wanted to build on that experience to develop a second career. One of the vendors she had had some dealings with during her final years in government offered her a job selling to the same offices she'd just retired from. She thought it would be easy because she would know the people in her old office and was familiar with their procurement procedures—but that wasn't the case. In the interim, a change of presidential administrations brought new management, a lot of old-timers retired, and she faced a new landscape. The advantage she had was that she knew what level and kind of procurement should happen in that government office; she made a list of things that, once known, would give her situational awareness. A checklist of knowns and unknowns helped her establish information requirements and a strategy for selling to the new occupants of "her" old office.

When I described the process of "reading in" that an officer assigned to a new station goes through, that is also a planned technique to aid situational awareness. There is a built-in advantage to the host country because its agents see us come and go. First, there was station chief Harry for three years; everybody liked Harry. Then Joe stayed for two years; nobody liked Joe. The host country has learned our idiosyncrasies as a station team and even has seen how a change in the dynamics affects our work. They are the home team, so we go in with a tremendous disadvantage. We are constantly the visiting team. The more we prepare and then keep our antennae tuned, the better.

HOW DO YOU GET ACTIONABLE INTELLIGENCE?

In collecting information, identify the needs and tools:

- Specify the information you need.

- To the best of your ability, determine who has it or where it resides.

- Create a plan to get it.

- Stay open to unexpected sources and have a system for integrating new data points into your picture.

- When a collection technique works—or a behavior pattern affecting a collection technique works—share it with colleagues.

- Ask questions wherever you go. And then listen.

CHAPTER **SIX**

. . . .

Collection—Interpersonal Skills

A case officer primarily meets people of interest and works one-on-one to determine if they have the access the officer is seeking, and if they are open to cooperating covertly to provide information. Equally, what would it take to elicit their cooperation? If I break down the occupations in the world into five basic categories—teach, make, fix, persuade, and uplift— then I would say that the dominant category for a case officer is persuade. That makes the officers first cousins to people in sales, motivational speaking, politics, and criminal law, among others. They have to have good interpersonal skills in order to be successful; as a general rule, the sharper those skills, the more they achieve the goals.

What I've learned about human behavior and information collection using a range of interpersonal skills derives almost entirely from my years in the Clandestine Service. I build on that here to indicate how a company might organize itself to improve collection activities, both through face-to-face and through nonpersonal means.

COLLECTING INFORMATION ON PEOPLE

When a case officer meets someone who might be of interest later, he records mentally—and then in writing—descriptive information to give

121

the most useful guidance possible to another officer. Does the person seem cynical? Naïve? Materialistic? Idealistic? Introvert? Extrovert? These are the traits that can affect that person's emotional state as the officer approaches the individual to cooperate covertly with the American government. They would also make note of other distinguishing aspects, such as any nervous gestures or distinctive scars.

In building the profile of such a person, the case officer has to be able to arrive at a complete picture, from the externals of appearance and mannerisms to the internals of the importance of religion. It reminds me how the dramatist Henrik Ibsen described his development of characters, in his famous essay "The Primacy of Character." In the first draft of a play, he knew as much about a character as if he'd chatted with him on a train ride. In the second draft, it was as though he had spent a few weeks in a spa with the person. And by the third draft, he knew the character intimately.

As a case officer, I would capture my observations and impressions in a report that would, it was hoped, be useful to me and my colleagues or to another case officer years later, even if there had been no contact with the individual in the intervening time. The idea was to provide information that would help someone else get to know the target on as many levels as possible. Usually, over time, these reports would come together to create a picture of a person, much like Ibsen's second draft of a play. With the active cultivation of that person over time, we might finally get to the third-draft level of knowledge.

Companies have their own system for obtaining and recording information, and they commonly rely heavily on Web-based technology. For example, when you search online for information, the keywords that you enter, the sites visited, and the dates and times of those visits find a way into the records of Microsoft, Google, or Yahoo!, depending on the search engine you use. At the time of this writing, Microsoft had saved those records for eighteen months; Google retained them for nine months; Yahoo! held them for "only" three months. The average user may assume there's an anonymity factor, but don't.

You are being profiled, in a sense, just as a case officer begins building a profile of someone met in person. Interests, purchases, and even intentions take shape as a result of your Internet use. Do a search for flights to

Las Vegas, if you want to test the system. If any of the sites you searched has your e-mail address—say, because you asked to be told when the cost of flights goes down—you will soon get e-mails offering you deals on hotels, cars, and show tickets. Maybe some of those deals look good, so you book with an airline and then buy some tickets to Cirque du Soleil. And then you book a hotel, which offers you a package deal for meals that you accept. If someone wanted to track you during your Las Vegas stay, it would be fairly easy. You are being tracked; in a commercial sense, you are being spied on.

When you do online shopping at Christmastime, you allow companies to build profiles of you, too. How you pay for your purchases, what you buy, where you ship it—you are much more than an anonymous customer.

Since this is a business book, let's turn the scenario around, because you are mostly likely the person who is seeking the information. Before going into what categories of information make a difference in forging a relationship with someone, let's look at the answer to, "Why bother collecting as much relevant information as possible on your potential or current customers?"

THE REWARDS OF COLLECTION

In a January 31, 2009, article for *Newsweek*, Christopher Dickey, author of *Securing the City: Inside America's Best Counterterror Force—The NYPD*, credited police commissioner Ray Kelly with moving toward a force that mirrors the diversity of New York City. Dickey noted that 40 percent of residents are foreign born, but Kelly had inherited a police force that did not include a mix of nationalities. In fact, he even surfaced a criticism of "Cold War–style background checks (that) often eliminated recruits who had been born overseas."

Significantly, Kelly's intelligence chief is a former senior CIA analyst who rose to head the Clandestine Service (CS), Dave Cohen. Dave is a very interesting figure, almost as well known for his coarse language as for his managerial innovations. His appointment to head up the CS raised eyebrows, but Agency leadership readily discerned that Cohen thought operationally. A few years after his stint in Agency operations, he was selected to head up the new intelligence unit of the NYPD, where he has gained a reputation for his hard-driving and imaginative leadership. Among the results is an NYPD that now includes officers who speak dozens of languages—up to forty-five by the year 2002—and represents multiple cultures. They understand street dialects of Pashto or Spanish, and can blend into a gang of thugs from Bangladesh as easily as a gang from Canton, Ohio.

Of course, recruitment of multilingual people is much easier for the NYPD, which has local law enforcement as its priority rather than national security interests abroad. The NYPD did something beyond the externals, though, that gives them an immeasurable edge. They went beyond having people with language skills and were invested in true diversity. If you want to collect intelligence, you need more than ears that understand and mouths that speak and skin tones that match your targets' (the latter being not that important, in many cases). You need a deep grasp of the other person's culture.

The payoff has been a real enhancement of the city's security defense against potentially devastating terrorist attacks. For example, in 2003, a Persian-speaking officer confronted two Iranians as they photographed a subway line beneath the East River. They left the country. In his *Newsweek* article, Dickey also reported that "a young undercover officer born in Bangladesh penetrated a small group of angry young immigrants, two of whom had started plotting to blow up targets in Staten Island and the subway station at Herald Square." The NYPD was in a position to exploit a success like this to spawn good publicity, whereas in many cases the CIA is not. Covert operations that succeed often must remain covert.

THE ARTS OF TRANSLATION

The myriad ways you can offend someone whose culture is foreign to you can derail a business deal, and you may not even realize what went wrong. Therefore, it is critical to know as much as possible about someone before trying to transact business, so that you have a sense of what's appropriate and most effective. In 1995, Bill Richardson, then a congressman from

New Mexico, went to Iraq in an attempt to extricate a couple of American hostages. While meeting with Saddam Hussein, he crossed his legs and flashed the sole of his shoe. To Saddam Hussein, that was like Richardson dropping his drawers and mooning him.

Language and cultural translations may be the most overtly difficult, but nuanced verbal communications in the same language or idiosyncratic body language can also create the need for interpretative skills. Something as basic as the way people sort information can lead to misunderstandings. Have you ever tried to negotiate a deal with someone who gets hung up on the precise flow of information, and interrupts your patter with questions? It's possible that you have a way of sorting information that puts it into big chunks first, and then you go into details later—like providing a table of contents before you explore the topics. Some people find that annoying. Once you introduce a topic, they want you to delve into it before going on to the next piece. It's almost like speaking two different languages. In collecting information from people, you have to listen for those differences.

Body language also varies in ways that I've observed through the years, but I never codified what I observed. My knowledge base was grounded in intuition and empirical "research." But if you want to explore this idea further, Greg Hartley's *I Can Read You Like a Book* and *The Body Language Handbook* do codify the steps to understanding and using body language. The process starts with paying attention to the individual and not making assumptions based on what you do and what you believe about the meaning of the person's movements or speech pattern—or even the way the person dresses. All of those characteristics make up what we call "body language." Observe the person in a relaxed state, or at least when there's minimal stress present; that's how you get a baseline. Since the next steps fill a book or two, here are just a handful of points that Greg makes.

First, determine if stress is present. When someone is uncomfortable for any reason—he's trying to deceive you, she finds you attractive, you brought up something embarrassing—that person's body language leaks signals of stress. Once you know how the person behaves and speaks when there's little or no stress present, you can spot the presence of it. A couple of signs to look for are these:

- Petting gestures if the person is a woman and rubbing gestures if it's a man. Women tend to stroke the neck, arms, earlobes, and so on, or maybe gently rub their fingers together if they are a little nervous. A man's stress gestures tend to be a bit firmer, like rubbing hands together or rubbing things. When you make these gestures, you invest energy in making yourself more comfortable.

- Sudden changes in the way the person moves or speaks. Maybe the person's speech slows down or speeds up a lot, or there's a noticeable difference in the way the person points or stands.

When you're collecting information from someone and you see these signs of stress, you need to do something differently to make that discomfort subside. Even worse signs would be those of "fight or flight," which include a lot of uncontrollable responses like pupils dilating and skin going pale. In theory, the skin goes pale because all the blood is moving to muscles that might either attack you or send the person running in another direction. Let's hope you never see this in a business situation.

Then again, you might see the pupils dilate and the person start to mirror your posture and the way you move. Maybe the face looks a little fuller, especially the lips. Time to move in and close the deal. This is someone who finds you attractive, or at least finds your ideas attractive. Similarly, reverse that. When you find yourself mirroring and know you're a bit flushed, your body is expressing a connection with the person, either deliberately or involuntarily. Ask yourself the tough question: Are you still in control or are you now vulnerable?

The next area of human communication that might require translation abilities is topics of interest. What if the target of your collection activities loves horseracing, or hunting, or gambling, and you know absolutely nothing about the topic? You have to engage the person in a way that enables you to learn enough to tighten the connection through better and better questions. In Section 2, I take a close look at operational tools and techniques that help you get this job done. They are remarkably like those used by top sales professionals.

Even without knowing those techniques or having the time to use them, you can collect relevant assumptions about a person that you can put to the test later. For example, let's say your source admits to enjoying gambling; the pleasure of winning seems to be an addictive need. Here is a person who may not be above cutting corners in order to get the satisfaction he needs.

If I were handling an agent like that, I would strongly suspect that he has no problem playing people against one another for profit. I'd expect him to inflate expenses, escalate his value to me, and string out his involvement in any operation where he might profit because he wants to be a financial winner in this game. The same can be said for business.

THE ARTS OF DECODING

A case officer has to do the translation quickly, to know whether someone is doing what he should be doing versus what he is doing. These are not aspects of behavior or personality that necessarily would be of concern in a business transaction, but there are analogous concerns of "walking the line." For instance, does this person display brand loyalty, as evidenced by purchasing tickets through Travelocity.com on a repeated basis? In many cases, "brand loyalty" is just another name for "change averse." If you're a competitor, this tidbit tells you that you have to go to extraordinary lengths to get the person to change—but once changed, as long as you deliver consistently on your promises, you have a reasonably good chance of establishing a long-term relationship. And if you have secured this profile information and are not a competitor, then you also have a path to establishing a relationship and sustaining it: Lure the customer, deliver on promises, and don't mess up. If you do that, then even lower prices or a more attractive set of deliverables may not lure away your change-averse customer.

We have on our staff psychologists and psychiatrists to provide professional insights that supplement a case officer's own direct observations, as well as notes from previous case officers regarding the individual. For example, as a case officer I could develop a personality assessment of someone and then take my notes to one of them to get professional insights. What does it mean that this person strokes her neck whenever I mention her family? (Sign of stress.) Is there a possible psychological reason he's frequently clearing his throat? (Sign of stress.) In covert operations, we are always looking for behaviors and action that are different— beyond the norm in one way or another. Similarly, in business you are always looking for behaviors and actions that are the same— that conform with what you expect—maybe too much so.

There are a number of ways you can direct the conversation to collect useful information. Returning to the example of the change-averse customer, if you are engaging the person face to face rather than tracking him electronically, focus on topics like residence, career, and food. You will pick up hints, or even obvious signals, about whether the person seems to embrace change and new adventures or finds the status quo more appealing. Someone who admits to relocating voluntarily, veering off in different career directions depending on opportunity and circumstances, and who "eats anything at least once," probably sees change as a positive condition or at least adjusts to it more agilely than a lot of other people.

Customers also give strong signals about their predisposition to complain and criticize, or to minimize problems. Conversations about health, consumer goods, and relationships often bring out their true nature. If the person is sick or a member of the family is sick, pay attention to how they deal with adversity: Is the person a victim, or is the condition something that represents a challenge? Talk of anything, from cars to laundry soap, can bring out the complainer in almost anyone, but try to determine if the tone is that of a victim or of a justifiably angry consumer who suspects that the solution is to switch brands—and will do it. Conversation will not only give you insights into a person's tendency to gripe but also how respectful the person is of private information. Someone who bemoans the fact that his wife no longer dresses up for him or pays attention to his needs is giving you *too much information*, regardless of whether a couple of cocktails influenced the admission.

You also want to know how confrontational someone is in assessing a potential relationship, whether it's a foreign agent or a customer. Talk about politics and social issues, and see where that goes. If you don't want to divulge your own beliefs to spark the conversation, ask a question. Someone who doesn't back off from a divisive remark, likely because his ideology is strong, is likely to be as assertive and judgmental about a lot of other things as well. Go from politics to beer, for example. Ask him what he sees as the difference between a good and bad beer—you may hear the same kind of committed and deliberate opinion.

Similarly, you want to assess an individual's passion—that is, what fuels her energy and strong, positive emotions. Until you find out what's really important to a person, you don't have a rounded picture of her personality. Talk about family, art, religion, medicine, or any other topic, and see what not only triggers animation but also initiates meaningful conversation. A person's passion will drive her to learn more about what it takes to be competent and respected in that area.

And if you want to do a deal with someone, whether it's buying a house or infiltrating an embassy, you want to know that the person can follow through on the project. If he feels passionate about literature and wants to publish a novel, but never writes anything, you might wonder how many of the individual's other "passions" are unfulfilled.

Human beings are full of surprises, of course. I may experience you as kind, a good listener, and even conciliatory—except when you play tennis. You're vicious and you lie when you feel you can get away with it. Different behaviors surface in different environments, and that reveals a person's personality. In essence, even if I don't create a situation that tests you, I observed it and it will most certainly have an effect on how I deal with you. That is why a profile does not take complete shape until you have experienced a person in different environments. As a corollary, two individuals experiencing the same person in different environments might have dramatically different ways of characterizing the individual. The stern director of marketing might be playful, even openly affectionate, when she's at home with her kids.

To construct a reliable picture of your target, therefore, you may want to draw the individual deliberately into situations where contrasting behaviors might show up. Let him drive you somewhere during rush hour. Take him on a boat trip. Play golf with him. Invite him to lunch at a down-home diner or an upscale restaurant.

Of course, if you're going to go to all this trouble, the person probably represents either an enormous investment or an enormous opportunity. This is someone you might put in charge of a billion-dollar division of your company, or someone who can write the annual check for $50 million in hardware upgrades and support services. Therefore, go all the way in learning about him. You want to know how the person acts toward you, who his colleagues are, and even something about his spouse. You want to know if he behaves differently with men and women, young and old, waiters and doormen.

The Agency didn't give case officers a checklist with thirty-nine items on it and say, "Go build a profile around these." The possibilities are endless, so focus on the traits that you think are fundamental to making your business relationships work. Codify the traits for yourself, and make decisions that are consistent with your criteria. This does not mean you ignore your gut reaction to someone, however. The objective assessments you make may well give you more reason to trust your gut—or they may help you retune your judgment. The following table should be useful in this effort.

Selected traits that affect your style of recruitment (negotiation, sales, interviewing...)	When you detect it, verify: Manage the exchange(s) to see/hear if it surfaces again
Change averse	References and noticeable signs suggest ways of doing things, style of dress, and other easily controllable behaviors haven't changed in a long time. Can you create a mental link to his status quo to get your message across?
Victim mentality	It's always someone else's fault. If anything goes wrong in this business arrangement, it will be your fault. Is there someone else you can deal with? Someone who doesn't have a scapegoat for every problem?

Confrontational	If everything seems to be a hot-button issue, then maybe he just habitually pushes back. There's a lot of energy there: Can you stand on the same side of a big issue and use that energy to your advantage?
Passionate	When it's clear he cares a lot about something, show interest and respect. Don't try to steer the conversation away from it with your agenda; pay attention to see how his strong interest dovetails with your message.

GETTING INSIDE COMMUNICATIONS

The way that companies gain access to privileged information is often by giving their employees the technical skills to listen well. A corollary skill is knowing how to keep the conversation going somewhere.

In the Clandestine Service, when someone becomes an agent, the case officer may grow closer to him than anyone else in the world because the officer knows the agent's darkest secret—that he is cooperating with a foreign power to provide information about his country. In some cases, the officer is closer than a spouse, because the agent is the sole person he has confided in. The officer becomes mother, father, spouse, confessor—the relationship between an agent and a case officer is extraordinarily close.

Often, when there's this type of close relationship, the person speaks out of school because he trusts the other not to misuse the information. Sometimes the best way to put that person at ease is with a *quid pro quo*: You cross over the line slightly, divulging some personal opinions or information, so that he feels more comfortable about his vulnerable admission. Each of you demonstrates a measure of confidence and trust.

In one instance, I was handling a terrorist. In our discussions, which were often quite protracted, he wanted to talk about American policy. I did that, and in doing so, I went beyond what would have been considered the official line. He appreciated that; it helped to maintain his confidence in me. I wasn't giving away secrets. I was just giving an opinion about some bit of American politics. But he valued that and demonstrated his trust by continuing to serve as a reliable source.

Similarly, the *quid pro quo* model guides business conversations in many venues and in many ways. A friend of mine told me of an industry conference where a representative of Microsoft introduced himself by saying, "I'm from Microsoft and we're taking over the world!" People threw balls of paper at him, but all in good fun. He was a really likeable guy. Three people from different companies invited him to join them later for dinner and drinks. Afterward, one of them had this sense of "uh, oh." After the Microsoft guy blurted out some criticisms of his company, this woman found herself divulging things about her company that she shouldn't have. A clear case of "too much information" haunted her. What did the Microsoft man do with it? Who knows?

There's another way to look at this, however. From the point of view of those other people in the room, Mr. Microsoft's deviation from the company line may be an indication of his willingness to serve as a source for them. It's not automatic. It's not as though one of those people could take him out to the parking lot and say, "By the way, would you like to spy for me?" But one of them might say on the side, "You have interesting insights. Want to have drinks tomorrow?" He could then see how authentic and deep the dissatisfaction really is.

In the world of technology there are many forums in which people exchange technical information for the purpose of solving joint problems that are hurting their sales or undermining customer satisfaction. One of the generic, common problems is the noninteroperability of software products. Your stuff doesn't work with my stuff, so we use the neutral ground of a trade association or consortium to create a "safe" environment where we can figure out how to fix that. Theoretically, the software engineers who do this work abide not only by their own companies' rules of what may or may not be disclosed but also by the rules of the organization creating that safe environment.

These same people are not bound by the rules of that neutral organization at trade shows, however, or at other ad hoc encounters in which technical matters might take center stage in a conversation. Add a few cocktails to the conversation and suddenly you might have confidential discussions aired in public places. So companies would be smart to tell their people to avoid the pitfall of divulging sensitive information, but they would be just as smart to tell them how to get as much information as possible that would be useful to the company.

Case officers are trained in elicitation techniques, and the more seasoned ones draw from their experience gathered in years of meeting with foreigners abroad. The techniques for effective and productive interactions with people can be found in such classics as Dale Carnegie's *How to Win Friends and Influence People*, or *Get People to Do What You Want* by interrogation instructor Gregory Hartley.

In business, your technique for obtaining information will be shaped by whether you want an operational relationship or just a quick bit of information from someone you may never see again. Some of the options include:

- Bone-throwing—that is, giving information in order to get it. In the course of talking with your potential source, you could mention a proposal someone made at a staff meeting. You know the proposal was shot down, but you don't address that fact. When you talk about something that seems to be confidential, that sense of *quid pro quo* often takes hold.

- Being deferential about the other person's expertise. It's human nature to want to feel smarter, sexier, more resourceful than another person. Offer an opinion on how to do something that's inadequate, for example, and then let the compliments flow when the person who "knows better" gives you more details on his innovations than you had ever hoped for.

• Bringing up a topic and then just listening—endlessly. More often than not, if you were to record conversations of mine, especially when I first meet someone, the other guy is doing most of the talking. And he's probably talking about himself, what he thinks, how he would do something. It's a lifelong habit of mine from the field to let people enjoy the sound of their own voice.

ELICITATION TECHNIQUES

I draw a sharp distinction between elicitation and interrogation. Interrogation is associated with questioning persons in unfriendly circumstances; elicitation is what case officers do in the normal course of socializing, as we develop contacts, assess individuals as possible sources, and keep up with the local scene. Nevertheless, the techniques of both can be described in exactly the same terms as long as we are talking about the psychological interrogation techniques perpetrated by World War II German interrogator Hanns-Joachim Gottlob Scharff. For Scharff, interrogation was a conversation. His methods, which never involved physical means to elicit information, were adopted by the U.S. military after the war. The focus was on understanding the psychology of why people connect with others in conversation and what someone can do to trigger the desire to connect quickly.

Earlier in this chapter I presented ways to establish a connection with someone to secure information, as well as ways to probe the individual's personality. The science of interrogation codifies those ways as psychological "approaches." In layman's terms, they involve techniques such as flattery, criticism, and using the leverage of someone's emotions. These interrogation techniques can be put to work an office—say, for example, between a manager and a member of the staff:

• *Direct Questioning.* What signs did you notice that the deal was falling apart?

• *Incentive.* If you give me a full report on exactly who did what to make this project fail, you'll earn a Christmas bonus.

- *Emotional Appeal.* Your concern for your team has always been evident, so just do what's best for them. Tell me what went wrong so everyone can learn from it.

- *Fear Up.* If you don't tell me who's to blame for the project failure, I'll find someone to blame and there will be hell to pay.

- *Fear Down.* You seem very upset about the failure of the project. Don't worry. Just calm down and we'll figure this out and fix the problems.

- *Pride and Ego Up.* You do a great job, day after day. This project failure is an anomaly. Let's do a thorough postmortem and I'm sure something like this will never happen again.

- *Pride and Ego Down.* I think you've been slipping lately, but maybe other members of the team are making you look bad. Tell me exactly what happened with this project.

- *Futility.* I don't see any way for you to get out of this mess without your career taking a hit. Why don't you tell me what happened with the project. Maybe I can make some sense of it.

- *We Know All.* A few of the team members have sent me e-mails about the project, so I have a pretty good idea of what went on. Tell me what you think happened here.

- *Rapid Fire.* What happened with this project? Where did it go off track? How long have you suspected there was a problem? Who the heck is to blame for this travesty, anyway?

- *Silence.* Have a seat. Let's talk about the project. [The manager says nothing after this, simply waiting for the employee to start blurting things out because silence is awkward.]

Donald P. Gregg (2009), a former case officer who served with the Agency for thirty years, said in his article "Speaking with the Enemy," the "key to successful interrogation is for the interrogator—even as he controls the situation—to recognize a prisoner's humanity, to understand his culture, background and language. Torture makes this impossible." The substance of this applies to every business transaction: Understanding your audience makes you more effective than an intimidating display.

CONNECTING WITH PEOPLE TO COLLECT INFORMATION OF VALUE

- Go where your targets go, whether it's in person or in cyberspace.

- Look for patterns of behavior and speech; deviations from that will alert you to a change in the person's state of mind.

- Take language, culture, and context into consideration. Don't project your own background and circumstances on others when trying to understand them.

- Note if you see stress present when you bring up a particular topic. Use your tone of voice and other body language to reduce the stress and facilitate a connection.

- When your target gets excited, figure out what caused it: Competitive spirit? Concern about confronting something new? Anger over being victimized? Passion for an idea?

- If possible, interact with the person in multiple environments.

- Listen everywhere. Tune in especially well in any environment where your targets are.

CHAPTER SEVEN

Analysis

Why would information gathered solely from open sources earn a classification of confidential and be packaged as intelligence? The answer lies in a story that Greg Hartley, decorated U.S. Army interrogator and interrogation instructor, and whose books on human behavior are mentioned in Chapter 6, told me about creating an interrogation scenario. Hartley, who taught at the SERE (Survival, Evasion, Resistance and Escape) school, used various sources on the Web to pull together something he thought represented a realistic scenario in which U.S. military personnel might find themselves. It was too realistic for the brass, who told him that it could not be used. Having had front-line exposure to situations, proficiency in Arabic, and a wealth of experience in teaching both interrogation and resistance to interrogation, his ability to read between the lines of publicly available information enabled him to create a document that could earn a classification requiring a clearance to read.

The ability to turn the words of whatever source into intelligence depends on the person doing the analysis. A human activity, analysis is done by people. Computers can sort information in myriad ways, which is a good first step in the analysis process, but the scrutiny of that information needs a human brain.

Newsweek's decision to reinvent itself, announced in an article by Kathleen Deveny (2009), reflects the fact that new sources pelt us with information like a never-ending thunderstorm. The premium is now on high-caliber analysis. In discussing how the magazine hopes to utilize the talents of "the best writers and thinkers," Deveny noted, "while there is no shortage of information out there, we believe there is a scarcity of insights" (pp. E2, E4).

Just as "key judgments" influencing policy decisions may arise out of freely available documents, many companies have shaped competitive advantages out of each other's brochures, press releases, and executive speeches. Entire companies have been established based on the vision of someone who looked at the marketplace and, instead of seeing a crowded landscape, saw gaps in the landscape.

Quang X. Pham, founder of Lathian Systems, showed that kind of perception when he submitted an idea to the Hummer Winblad Venture Partners' February Madness. The idea was for the world's first virtual drug-representative portal. (The event had been March Madness until the NCAA called "foul" for copyright infringement.) Pham won $5 million as a result of presenting an idea that reflected solid intelligence about the marketplace—intelligence that someone else could easily have gotten if he had looked in the right place and used some imagination.

A friend of mine has made a fortune by collecting marketing intelligence. He visits with doctors, collects their ideas about devices that would be useful in their practice, and then develops them into working models, which he takes to the companies that can build and sell the products. He is not a hammer-and-saw guy, nor is he a software guy. He is a listener and a recorder, who then takes the information given to him and processes it. He doesn't offer raw thoughts from doctors to his company contacts; he presents the concepts so that it is clear how they meet the requirements of a market segment.

APPROACHES TO ANALYSIS

Analysis falls into two types: solitary and Socratic. The brilliant introvert, with fingers flying over the keyboard, breaks codes in e-mails and sees details in aerial photos that no one else sees. That's the movie version of an Agency analyst, and for once, the characterization is spot-on in many cases. The Agency does attract geniuses to the analyst corps, and they may well be people who like to work alone. The Agency also values the mix of viewpoints and insights that come from people jointly analyzing information.

The Socratic method is an approach to learning through questions and answers, with the underlying assumption that the people engaged in the exchange have some differences of opinion. You can do it with a single team, or you can create a couple of teams to analyze the same raw material.

The distinction I draw between brainstorming and analysis as a team activity is that the first is a response to circumstances and the second is an assessment of circumstances. For example, the Agency can face the same problem as any company in allocating its resources to conduct analysis: the tyranny of the urgent. But since the Agency's product is intelligence, we have to do what it takes to make sure the analysis occurs.

When faced with issues of huge national importance, there is a deliberate effort in the Intelligence Community to foster competing circles of analyses—an A Team versus B Team approach to analyzing the same information. If in business you use this approach, make sure the composition of your teams reflects diverse points of view. I have heard from friends in the publishing industry that a decision whether to handle a book, or how to handle a book, comes down to the analysis of the marketing team versus the judgment of the editorial team. What good is that? The result of those conflicting schools of analysis is so predictable it's worthless. You want teams composed of experts who do not have the same priorities or backgrounds, but they should have similar talents and experience.

There is always room for dissenting views and, in fact, they are encouraged. The aim is not to achieve homogeneity but, rather, to capture those dissenting views and offer them along with the conclusions of the majority, in much the same way as the Supreme Court documents how the

Justices in the minority came to a different conclusion than their majority-voting colleagues.

Make sure everyone contributes something when you use this process. The Agency could probably make the same assertion as many large companies could make: Within the organization, you can find a true expert about anything that's relevant to its operation. So, to do the best job of setting up teams for the analysis, find that person and invite him to speak. Not everyone is comfortable speaking to a group; the default position for introverts is often to defer to people who are more persuasive, regardless of their expertise. So someone in the group with a nonthreatening persona and the ability to ask solid questions needs to request the input. That then is followed by a recap, both to reinforce that person's contribution and to open the door to additional details and clarifications.

The information that emerges from meetings like this leads to a decision. It is never intended to justify a decision that has already been made. For example, the Agency does not seek information for the purpose of affirming preexisting theories. Any company operates that way does so at its peril. One of the flaws that became evident in the midst of the dot-com heyday was that some young companies rushed a product or service to market and then used market intelligence to create consumer interest, instead of using marketing intelligence to design a product that people needed and wanted. This information spin rather than information analysis is one of the factors that led to the collapse of the dot-com era. Relying on an approach like that is like designing and building a bomber with superior firepower, and then concluding, "Gosh, guess we have to find an enemy now so we can use it."

FACTORS AFFECTING ANALYSIS

The Agency has *precedence indicators* on field communications to Headquarters that alert the recipient to how time-sensitive and important the information is. Whereas normal traffic has no indicators, something with a measure of urgency would be marked "priority"; something more pressing is marked "immediate." The extreme is "flash," which requires instant attention. Organizational politics seem to be the sole source of any system of precedence in many private-sector companies. That is, if you have a decision maker's ear and favor, your input moves to priority status faster than a colleague's.

When the Headquarters watch office gets a "flash" message, it then makes the decision about whether or not to wake the division chief, alert the director, or even notify the White House. Information at this juncture is at a critical point. What someone in the field sees as an "immediate" communication might be perceived quite differently by the Headquarters watch officer. Analysts serve a vital role, thus, in spotting the significance, or lack thereof, of the information from the field and mission requirements. When analysis is missing or weak at this juncture, disasters can occur.

In her book, *Pearl Harbor: Warning and Decision*, Roberta Wohlstetter (1962) discusses the plethora of information that indicated that Japan was a threat and was within striking distance of the United States. She asserts that, despite having good intelligence, the United States took no action to avert the attack because of a "failure of imagination." That is, no one in power believed that Japan would actually bomb U.S. territory.

Consider how easy it is to commit a failure of imagination in business if everyone on your team agrees with each other most of the time, has a similar background, reads the same books, and so on. If people working on the same project exhibit homogeneity, you probably won't get analysis that runs counter to the norm, like "Maybe we should consider that Japan might bomb Hawaii."

In a report by a review panel composed of four senior officers (Armstrong, 1984), this type of error earned the label "consensus intelligence." The report looked at how the hazards of single-outcome forecasting led to poor intelligence judgments and flawed recommendations about the so-called Sino-Soviet split, the Soviet development of the ALFA nuclear submarine, Muammar Qadhafi's takeover in Libya, OPEC's December 1973 increase in the price of oil, the revolutionary transformation of Ethiopia, the Soviet invasion of Afghanistan, and the destruction of

Shah Mohammad Reza Shah Pahlavi's regime in Iran. If the report had been written in this century, it no doubt would have included the near-universal estimates by intelligence agencies that Saddam Hussein had weapons of mass destruction (WMD).

The lessons learned here centered on the fact that the problems associated with the flawed analyses were not random or divergent; the panel saw "recurrent common factors": "This addiction to single-outcome forecasting defied both estimative odds and much recorded history. It reinforced some of the worst analytical hazards—status quo bias and a prejudice toward continuity of previous trends, 'playing it safe,' mirror-imaging, and predispositions toward consensus intelligence."

The authors of this report also relied on a British term to describe another problem: *perseveration*. They defined this as a tendency to allow judgments made in the early stages of an evolving situation to influence later analysis. Essentially, it's getting stuck in what you conclude early on and then finding data to support that theory. Anyone familiar with the criticisms of the U.S. incursion into Iraq has heard this argument as it applies to "evidence" of weapons of mass destruction.

In the corporate sector, high-profile attorney Marc S. Dreier's $700 million gain in selling fake notes provides a fascinating example of single-outcome forecasting. Until the discovery of his fraud in late 2008, savvy investors who met the wealthy lawyer with offices in Manhattan and Albany, New York; Los Angeles and Santa Monica, California; Pittsburgh, Pennsylvania;, and Stamford, Connecticut, saw what they wanted to see and what other people told them they should see: a brilliant and successful man who should be trusted. When he pretended to be other people, and enticed everyone from receptionists to CEOs to believe in his stature and ability, he set up and perpetuated an acceptance scenario—the picture of perseveration. In his excellent article for *Fortune*, Roger Parloff (2009) said in substance what the Agency's panel of investigators had expressed in their article: "The scam succeeded for as long as it did because none of his victims could conceive that anyone of Dreier's stature would act with such monumental recklessness, selfishness, and self-destructiveness."

STRATEGIC INSIGHTS

Let's say a case officer makes contact with a low-level government employee who happens to have access to sensitive documents. That employee gives the case officer a copy of those papers and returns to his job in the bureaucracy. He doesn't understand what he gave the case officer; he just knows it had something to do with a nuclear project. Contrast this with the same set of papers coming from the government official who put together the research team for the nuclear project. Along with the papers, he provides notes about the purpose of the project, how he chose the people on the team, what they will be doing next, and how much they got paid.

The first asset gave raw information that will be conveyed to analysts; the tendrils of its possible meanings could extend in many different directions. The second asset also provided strategic insights that gave the analysts context. Those insights streamlined the process of connecting the data points, so the analysts may have less need to spend time on interpretation and have more foundation for making recommendations. This is one reason, at least in the foreseeable future, that the Google search tool will not be replacing reference librarians, the specialists in finding written sources of information that those of us pre-Google people relied on.

In September 2008, John Taylor (essentially a reference librarian) died at the age of eighty-seven, after serving as a military specialist at the National Archives in Washington, D.C., for sixty-three years. The scholar-authors who produced books about intelligence activities, particularly related to the military, relied on Taylor a great deal. He was the source who understood how to match the material available to a researcher's requirements. One of those researchers was Ed Fishel, whose book *The Secret War for the Union: The Untold Story of Military Intelligence in the Civil War*, received high praise for its unique information and insights. The reviewer for *Library Journal* raved that, "Ed Fishel's scholarship is breathtaking." That scholarship was, in part, due to John Taylor, who took Fishel to a room in the National Archives that contained all of the collected Union Army intelligence reports of the Civil War, untouched since the end of the Civil War.

In business, the person with the strategic insights that you need may be someone outside your organization. It may be someone who understands your requirements, and then objectively takes the data points available and puts them into context to see how they fit together. Companies sometimes balk at the cost of hiring marketing, public relations, and other consultants because it's hard to assign a dollar value to strategic insight. But when the consultant is absolutely clear about how the requirements of a project relate to your mission, you have the potential to get an impressive return on investment.

In the late 1990s, a start-up technology company hired Maryann on a consulting basis to do marketing communications projects. When the marketing vice president asked her what she charged for writing copy, she told him it was $1/word. "Even for 'the'?" he shouted. She told him it applied to every single word in every single document. Despite his grumbling, he hired her. After doing her homework about the company, she wrote a seven-word tag line for the company's main product, among other things. It captured her take on the value of the company's Internet security product. The company featured the tag line in their ads and marketing material for years after that. During those years, whenever the vice president complained about her bill, she reminded him of that $7 investment.

Just as Maryann's insights produced long-term value in the form of a tag line, there were unexpected and continuing benefits that came out of Ed Fishel's research. With the resources John Taylor identified for him in the Archives, Fishel was able to document the contribution of the Bureau of Military Intelligence (BMI), which became America's first all-source reporting arm. They began reporting information from Confederate prisoners, spies they sent into camps, and even balloons—their nineteenth-century version of overhead surveillance. And based largely on that book, two senior analysts at the CIA have created something called a "staff ride." People can go to Gettysburg Battlefield and receive a narrated ride about events that occurred and decisions that impacted those events. I thought this had such value as a teaching tool that the core experience is now offered through the International Spy Museum.

The lesson offered by this experience is in the extent to which intelligence, or the lack of it, determined the results of that pivotal battle and other military confrontations. Its value at the International Spy Museum is as a powerful illustration of the value of intelligence to military decision making. It spotlights exactly why the Union knew what the Confederacy's strengths and weaknesses were in that battle. The Union's military leadership and senior government executives knew far and away more than their Confederate counterparts, and that intelligence provided the real ammunition for defeat. In business decisions, good intelligence will not be the only source of your victory, but the lack of it could be the source of your defeat. Smart business is rooted in much more than a quality product and comprehension of the marketplace. You have to know your competitors. You have to know what they can do, as well as what they have done. And then you can use that intelligence to your benefit.

MOVING YOUR INFORMATION TOWARD INTELLIGENCE

- A keen analyst can connect dots that no one else even sees. Be sure you always have someone like that—at least one person—on your team.

- Don't confuse brainstorming with analysis.

- In using a team approach to analysis, make sure the team is composed of people with different areas of expertise and points of view—not all marketing or all engineering, but a diverse group.

- Help your analysts set priorities by being clear about requirements: What intelligence is most important to the mission? What has the most urgency associated with it?

- Beware if you see yourself or others doing analysis coming to the same conclusions with different sets of information. The conclusions may be valid, but you might also be making assumptions based on past experiences and information rather than on what's facing you now.

- Cultivate healthy skepticism; it will improve your analytic abilities, as well as those of people around you. You won't undermine a culture of trust in your organization by doing that—you'll help strengthen it by not settling for superficial answers or handy solutions to problems.

CHAPTER EIGHT

Dissemination

Dissemination refers to the activity of packaging and distributing final products. In the Clandestine Service, intelligence is collected and produced in response to requirements. It is also incumbent on intelligence officers to provide intelligence that has not been asked for, but seems relevant if it's something that is believed policymakers need to know. The way the Agency does this has application to the world of business.

If a Clandestine officer is in the field, providing a report, the basic reporting criteria are date, location, source, summary, and detail. Intelligence reports reflect that information, but they may be consolidated with other contact reports, analyzed, and refined to produce something more useful to decision makers. As the information gets transformed into intelligence, all along the line and all the way up to something like a national intelligence estimate for the president, officers know that using some kind of standard for conveying the material helps decision makers use it. For instance:

- *Be specific in addressing the topic.* Don't wander off into sidebar material.

- *Be accurate.* If you insert something that reflects your opinion or intuition, make sure it's presented in such a way that your audience won't mistake it for a fact.

- *Organize the material so that the priority information appears up front.* You aren't writing a novel that's designed to draw the reader into a story so you can offer a punch line on a later page.

Similar considerations should be used in business communications. For example, what is a decision maker in a company supposed to know, and then act on, with a note like this from a person in the field?

> Great meeting with the client! Probably three or four things we could improve on. He also said the billing process is a little confusing, so I'll hand that one off to accounts receivable. His main problem is with the installation, but I'm not sure I agree with him. His other issue had to do with interoperability with other software they are running, but the truth is, all of our competitors have the same problem, so I don't think he'd leave us over it. I'll do a complete debrief at the weekly meeting on Friday.

This is all too common in the private sector. In contrast, here is an example of *formatted* information, albeit the highest level that the Intelligence Community provides, so it isn't exactly like a sales report. Although it would be nearly impossible to match the gravitas of the following document on Soviet military action—designed to help the president make decisions about military and political actions—it isn't that hard to organize other material based on this model. The following example is not something from the field, by a long shot; it's the cover sheet for a March 30, 1948, report by a joint ad hoc committee representing the CIA and the intelligence agencies of the State Department, Army, Navy, and Air Force.

The Problem

1. We have been directed to estimate the likelihood of a Soviet resort to direct military action during 1948.

Discussion

2. Our conclusions are based on considerations discussed in the Enclosure.

Conclusions

3. The preponderance of available evidence and of considerations derived from the "logic of the situation" supports the conclusion that the USSR will not resort to direct military action during 1948.

4. However, in view of the combat readiness and disposition of the Soviet armed forces and the strategic advantage which the USSR might input to the occupation of Western Europe and the Near East, the possibility must be recognized that the USSR might resort to direct military action in 1948, particularly if the Kremlin should interpret some U.S. move, or series of moves, as indicating an intention to attack the USSR or its satellites.

Take the poorly written note to the company executive from the man in the field, and use the joint committee's basic format; you might get something like this:

Subject: Meeting with XYX Client to determine level of satisfaction.

Discussion: Will deliver full report Friday; no action needed before then.

Conclusions: Client has some dissatisfaction with billing; will attempt to resolve by working with accounts receivable. Issues with installation and interoperability don't appear to be deal-breakers, but must be addressed with closer technical support.

This note is two-thirds the length of the original and delivers the same information, but in a more usable form.

Following is an example of what the president sees in his morning Presidential Daily Brief (PDB) from the Agency. This PDB for President Lyndon Johnson leads with information about Greece around the time I was stationed in that region. Note the order of presentation—an indication of the order of importance in terms of possible action.

Daily Brief
25 April 1967

1. *Greece:* The new government is anxious to be accepted by its NATO Allies. In talks with Americans, high officials have underscored their pro-US position, and the new foreign ministers lost no time in accepting an invitation to Adenauer's funeral. [This is followed by a redacted section.] The coup in Athens has created some uneasiness on Cyprus where Greek Cypriots in particular are not quite sure what may come next.

2. *South Vietnam:* Voters have now gone to the polls in 900 of the approximately 1,000 villages scheduled to elect their officials this spring. Total turnout so far has been 77 percent of those registered. Viet Cong harassment was light during the latest polling last Sunday.

3. *Soviet Union:* The ill-fated flight of *Soyuz-1* is a serious setback to the Soviet manned space program. The Russians are not likely to risk another cosmonaut fatality until they have made a detailed investigation of the disaster and corrected the technical difficulties that plagued colonel Kamarov's entire mission. Damage to the capsule will hamper such investigations.

4. *Communist China:* Chinese leadership below Mao Tse-Tung, Lin Piao, and Chow En-Lai has been changed drastically in the past month.

Leaders in current favor turned out for a rally on 20 April and again with Mao and Lin yesterday. Five important Polituburo members are missing, including foreign minister Chen Yi. Lin Piao's wife showed up at the rally along with Madame Mao, the perennial harridan of the Cultural Revolution.

The belated entry of these ladies into public life—both had been seldom seen and never heard before last year—suggests they are useful representatives at meetings their husbands do not care to attend.

Outside Peking, there is continued evidence of economic dislocation, although not on the scale that we saw in January.

5. *Indonesia:* Relations between Djakarta and Peking took another nose dive yesterday, but neither country seems willing to be the one to break diplomatic ties entirely, charging that the Chinese Embassy had organized antigovernment demonstrations. Indonesians threw the two most senior Chinese diplomats out of the country. Within hours Peking repaid in kind.

6. *Bolivia:* Bolivian troops have scored their first victories against the guerrillas. Twice last week Army patrols hit guerrilla bands, inflicting casualties and taking prisoners. Several foreign nationals were captured including a French Communist with Cuban connections who is something of a theoretician on guerila warfare. These recent victories should help pump up Bolivian Army morale.

By the time the policymaker gets a report like the above, a lot has gone on. A five-line paragraph has gone through multiple steps—collection, analysis, verification, and more of the same—to forge the cleanest statement of priority information possible.

Contrast this with the mess that many senior executives see in memos and you can realize how one supports decision making while the other can easily undermine it.

ELEMENTS OF THE PRESIDENT'S DAILY BRIEF

The Agency case officer's contact report is for the file, for the record, for the continuity of the operation. The reports officer at the station takes the intelligence that comes out of the meeting, writes in as clear and accurate a way as possible, and describes the source. What the analyst then gets does not contain the name of the officer who provided the original report, but some description of the source. The analyst then combines the intelligence in the report with pertinent material from all other available sources and creates a report. It's incumbent on the analyst to limit her judgments and conclusions to the content of the report.

The most important message you can take away from this is to create your report, whether written or verbal, specifically for your audience. Do not treat everyone within earshot, or in your e-mail address book, equally when you deliver information.

On occasion, the Agency made documentary-style videos to support briefings going to Ronald Reagan. His background was film, and he responded well to information carefully and accurately presented in that medium. On the other hand, Jimmy Carter delved into the details of many topics much more than you would expect a president to do, but he had trained as an engineer at the Naval Academy and had served as a submarine commander, a position requiring him to know intimately about every nut and bolt on his vessel. George H. W. Bush liked to have portions of the briefings on index cards so that he could look at them and think about them during the day.

Knowing your audience, therefore, is not just a matter of knowing the person's position in the organization. It's about knowing the individual's preference for processing new information, how it should be presented to maximize his comprehension and retention. For instance, one of the hallmarks of our age is its many open sources of good (and bad) information. During the Cold War, about 20 percent of the information the United States needed about the Soviet Union came from open sources, and we had to scramble to get the other 80 percent from human agents, satellites, electronic eavesdropping, and other covert means.

That situation has flipped in the twenty-first century. Now, about 80 percent of what intelligence analysts needs is available through open sources and we have to dig for the remaining 20 percent. Of course, the challenge of analysis remains—and is every bit as vital—because volume does not translate to quality. Analysts now have to navigate a river to find the five drops we really need.

The other part of this information-reporting process is that, as we give information, we take away new requirements. That is, what are the questions the decision maker asks as a result of getting that briefing? What grabs the person's interest and attention more than anything else?

MANAGING IMPERFECT INFORMATION

You don't want to seek the perfect at the expense of the good.

Information collection is done based on requirements; it is not random. Even though ongoing collection efforts may yield something that appears to be scrap metal, it may turn out to be gold. It's important, therefore, that whatever comes in is organized, but that only the information that contributes to meeting the requirements or conveys something new (the unknown unknowns) moves forward.

That salient information is combined with whatever else is available on the subject. CIA analysts deal with all-source reporting—everything from the secret reports provided by NCS officers to products from other Intelligence Community agencies to information available freely on the Internet. What they do then is something akin to fitting a jigsaw puzzle. They collect pieces, put them together, and make an intelligence estimate based on the incomplete picture that emerges. If the information added up to simply an array of facts, then we wouldn't need an intelligence estimate. The intelligence business exists precisely because we don't have all the facts; it's always about coming as close as we can to the facts. This has sometimes been referred to as *proximate reality*.

For instance, India has a nuclear capability. Once India set off a bomb, the intelligence requirement shifted to India's weapons-manufacturing capability. This levied a different reporting task on the field and on the analysts. In business, agilely refocusing efforts on meeting new information requirements puts a company way ahead of its competitors. The CEO or other senior executive who can identify those new requirements when no one else sees them taking shape deserves the big bucks.

In the early stages of what became known as the Cuban Missile Crisis, in October 1962, CIA and other Intelligence Community analysts, and even diplomats in Cuba, doubted that the Soviets would place nuclear missiles on the island. One voice dissented from the consensus, Agency Director John A. McCone, who was following the crisis from the South of France, where he was on his honeymoon. An engineer and successful businessman by background, he was new to the intelligence discipline, but he instinctively believed that the new Soviet surface-to-air missile (SAM) sites spotted around the island were there for a purpose—one being to discourage the United States from sending spy aircraft over the island. He was right, as the photographic intelligence (PHOTINT) from the ensuing flights would show.

During the Cold War, the United States needed to know the capabilities of the USSR and about its designs on the United States. What were they capable of doing to us? The big breakthrough in answering these questions came through data collection from satellites, not from human intelligence. We lost many recruited sources in our early efforts at HUMINT, so the urgency of developing a nonhuman way of getting the information we needed became a driving force in our scientific and technological projects. By the time we entered the Strategic Arms Limitation Treaty (SALT) talks, our negotiators had information that was far superior to what their Soviet counterparts had about their own country's capabilities. Even so, we didn't know everything and had to plan accordingly.

At one point, when I was chief of the staff dealing with the U.S. Senate, the Agency regularly informed the Senate Select Committee on Intelligence of the intelligence that was affecting the SALT talks. The director usually presented the data in closed sessions, testifying about "levels of confidence" concerning the nuclear weapons capabilities of the USSR. In other words, it was a matter of answering the question, "What's your level of confidence that they only have x number of weapons that are capable of hitting something within a 600-mile radius?" We would respond with a percentage based on analysis, like 80 percent.

The exercise of determining a level of confidence applies to any situation in which you don't have all the facts—and that's probably more often than situations in which you do have all the facts. As an example, take the disappearance on September 3, 2007, of businessman and adventurer Steve Fossett. Fact: He filled up his aircraft before he took off, and it holds 237 gallons of fuel. Fact: An aircraft like his gets a certain mileage, so his range of movement would be in an area defined by that range. Intelligence, but not fact: He said he was going in direction A and not direction B or C. So what was the level of confidence about where he might have crashed? Based on this information, it might have been 80 percent. In fact, we know now that a relatively high level of confidence was warranted because of where the body was found. More than a year after his death, a hiker found the crash site, obscured by rough terrain, in a Nevada desert, and DNA tests of bones in the area confirmed Steve Fossett's death.

Even using the sophisticated modeling software that exists today, with logic-tree rigor, we still do not have answers to some of history's more provocative and perplexing questions because we don't have enough of the right information. We don't know exactly what happened to Amelia Earhart, so we have to keep digging if we want to figure that out. We still aren't positive who Jack the Ripper was, regardless of the countless books and papers written on the topic. And so, we can say that the level of confidence about any given theory is only x percent—and that percentage can change from year to year, depending on the availability of new information.

Regardless of the arena in which you operate, if you have to deal with imperfect information and less than 100 percent odds, it's wise to allocate resources to contingency planning. Part of that process involves staying open to new information as it comes along. For my take on this, see Chapter 9, which covers "outcome thinking."

Indeed, entrepreneurs in fast-moving areas of high technology have no choice but to practice contingency planning. In the 1980s, some companies that had not conditioned themselves to respond effectively to new competitive information resorted to industrial espionage and reverse engineering to keep up. In a very famous case, IBM won $300 million from Hitachi in a civil suit related to the latter's acquisition of plans for a new computer disk drive.

Likewise, despite all of the engineering and market research poured into the development and roll-out of early personal digital assistants (PDAs), companies with substantial resources missed a fundamental fact about consumer preference. They did not plan for the reality that the good old-fashioned QWERTY keyboard would be a required element of a new generation of portable devices, rather than software that allowed you to scribble notes. The failure of products like Apple's Newton turned some key "unknowns" into "knowns," thereby providing a great opening for competing products.

DELIVERING AND ACTING ON TIMELY, ACCURATE, AND OBJECTIVE INFORMATION

- Structure your communications with requirements in mind.

- Use a presentation style that suits your audience and the purpose of your communication. A report to the CEO has a different look and feel from a request for assistance to a colleague.

- Since you will rarely have all the facts, set a threshold for how much intelligence you need to take action.

- Establish a level of confidence about the intelligence you have—50 percent? 80 percent?

- Even after determining a high level of confidence, allocate some resources and thought to contingency planning in case the unexpected occurs.

Organizational Improvement

The thrust of this section is on avoiding mistakes and/or learning from them. You don't want to have to scrap whatever you were doing and start over, nor do you want to salvage a dying project by putting it on endless life support.

. . . .

CHAPTER NINE

Public Image

For the first three decades of its existence, the CIA did not have an executive whose exclusive job it was to deal with the media or handle public relations. Considering it was a post-World War II, Cold-War era, it could be argued that there was no need for such a person. In general, Americans believed that intelligence activities were vital and, by necessity, were completely secret. That meant that the brand could be shaped by expectations rather than actual information. Many politicians accomplish this kind of branding success. Their whole persona is built on appealing to the expectations of the electorate, not on what they've actually done.

But there is a big difference between a brand created out of generally positive, unmanaged expectations—a combination of news coverage and circumstances working together to affect public opinion—and one created out of expectations managed by political strategists like Karl Rove and David Axelrod. Success or failure in strategic positioning shows up in the perception of your brand, and you would hope that you gave it a shape rather than allowed it to take shape.

Regardless of how open or closed the Agency has been in relating to the American public, as long as the connotation of the CIA's brand is "intelligence vital to our national security," then we're succeeding in communicating value—that is, as long as "intelligence" has the same meaning as the Agency assigns to it: timely, accurate, and objective information. In this chapter, I take a look at how and why that occurs, and how and why it does not.

ACCIDENTAL IDENTITY

Two main questions to ask yourself are: What elements converged to create the brand your organization now carries, and what do you gain by changing it? As a corollary to the latter, what would you change it to?

In one of the small towns in America where I've spent some time, there used to be three places that provided copying and printing services. As the technology improved, and the need for printing evaporated, competition became a war of the copiers. One of the businesses, which had primarily provided printing services, shut down. The other two continued head to head until one of them invested in high-end color and large-format equipment. The differentiation then became clear; it was no longer a matter of which one was conveniently located or who had the better prices. One company established itself as the place to go for specialty services, while the other, by default, became the place you went for everyday needs. One deliberately established a brand and the other was assigned a brand by its competition.

Our two main political parties in the United States try to do this to each other on a regular basis. For one election, the Republican Party's brand is "the change party" and for the next election, the Democratic Party is "the party of change." Whoever gets there early and with the best rhetoric claims the slogan—and the brand. And similarly, when companies try to build a brand they think is responsive to market needs, but don't do much to sustain it, the brand loses meaning quickly. One example is the airlines that promoted themselves as "low-cost." Concurrently, various carriers saw the market desire for discount fares and soon there were so many of them that the shared brand idea lost its distinction.

Allowing the competition to define you is a nonstrategy; any success you achieve will be due to their branding failure. A win by default is still a win, but you don't deserve any credit for it.

TOO NECESSARY TO BE UGLY

According to a 2007 poll by Rasmussen Reports, 57 percent of Americans have a favorable opinion of the CIA. The results were on a par with another Rasmussen poll from 2007, indicating that 58 percent have a favorable opinion of Microsoft. Both the Agency and Microsoft are doing a lot better than business in general. In the years since 1976, when Gallup began reporting on the perceived ethics of professions in the United States, business executives have never earned a slot among the top ten most ethical professions. One specific cut of that information was featured in a November 24, 2008, Gallup report, which stated that only 23 percent of Americans rate the honesty and ethical standards of bankers as very high or high—down 12 percentage points from 2007.

An integral part of the relatively favorable opinion that the public holds of both the Agency and Microsoft is that both are perceived as necessary, to some degree. Some people may feel they are necessary evils, but the operative word is necessary. That's a much better position to be in than where some Wall Street firms are, which people who lost their life savings in the debacle of 2008–2009 tend to view as evil and unnecessary.

The CIA brand affects peoples' behavior. It opens a lot of doors, but often for the mixed response I mentioned above. When I was in public affairs, I was asked to take on a number of outside tasks because of my background in the Clandestine Service, since it was believed that my long experience in the Agency's core discipline added a powerful measure of credibility. Most people outside of Washington, D.C., have never met a CIA officer, let along one who has recruited and managed secret agents and has conducted covert operations. FBI folks live next door, but not spies. Because we live in an open society, the CIA—and certainly its National Clandestine Service—are unsettling to some citizens. However, my status as an Agency representative with a verifiable office and phone number was reassuring.

Once, we had information that a prominent woman in the arts was being targeted for assassination in an Eastern European country. I went to New York City to visit her and her husband. She had no reason to believe anyone wanted to kill her, but she did, in fact, have a trip planned to Eastern Europe. She and her husband received me cordially, though neither had ever dealt with the Agency or any other intelligence agencies. For her, my demeanor and status as a senior CIA representative conveyed credibility and authority. Not only did she promptly cancel the trip but also she later contacted me at my Washington office to discuss her new plans to visit the same area. Her later trip went off without incident.

THE AUTHENTIC IMAGE

In the wake of a highly public failure, "too necessary to be ugly" doesn't work for the CIA or Microsoft, any more than "too rich to be ugly" works for an aging Hollywood movie star. Regardless of whether or not 9/11 was an intelligence failure, or Vista was a disappointing operating system, media and circumstances came into play and damaged the brands of both the Agency and Microsoft. For both, it became a case of "too poor to be attractive" and a question of, "What do you want the public to see when they look at you?"

The director of the CIA under President Obama, Leon Panetta, showed that defensively building a brand is not good enough. Early in his tenure, he went on the offensive, asserting to House Speaker Nancy Pelosi, who had criticized the Agency for deceiving her, that the CIA did then in her case, and does now, speak truth to power. Positive media coverage of his actions and public reactions helped refurbish the Agency brand as "intelligence vital to national security." Panetta's strategy was to lend his personal credibility to the Agency brand, much as Director William Webster did when he was selected by President George H. W. Bush to head the Agency after its image had been tarnished by the Iran-Contra affair.

Panetta has a strong personal brand, therefore he had the ability to revamp the image of the Agency at a critical time.

During the same time, what did Microsoft do to help its image? It launched the "I'm a PC" ad campaign, only to be beaten image-wise by the really cool guy who uses a Mac. Microsoft doesn't even make PCs, so the messaging had an embedded glitch in terms of authenticity. This event followed closely on the heels of CEO Steve Balmer's tarnishing its image for shareholders, if not the public, by dancing around an acquisitions deal with Yahoo! co-founder and CEO Jerry Yang. Yang, who did his company's image the same disservice, found himself part of a "succession planning" discussion shortly thereafter.

In contrast, former championship boxer George Foreman's role in a branding offensive gave appliance maker Salton Inc. an incredible boost. When he endorsed their grill—now known as the George Foreman Grill, even though it is still a Salton product—he conveyed a believable message that the grill was a manly tool with which men can work magic. Likewise, the public image of Virgin Group can be summed up in three words: Sir Richard Branson. CEO Stephen Murphy, who has a background in finance, runs the company, but it's the face of Branson and his competitive and adventurous spirit that define Virgin's brand.

Rebranding to create an authentic image is generally not an overnight exercise, and it is generally not the work of single individual, like Leon Panetta or George Foreman. Of course, a single individual—especially if the person is the CEO—can do a lot to undermine the exercise as well as advance it. You need to say:

Where you want to be

Where you are

What the path is between the two

And then you put every department and every employee on that path. This sounds like a straightforward matter, but I have seen company boilerplates in media releases reflect something inconsistent with the "new" company message.

A company with a battered image is like an alcoholic employee. You can stop drinking and turn your life around, but the belief that the "new You" is the "authentic You" will take a while to take root in people's minds. Constant reinforcement will do that, and any deviation from the new image can undo it.

So, you have to know how far you can go with the new you. When an oil company declares it works hard so people can go to the pump and fill the tanks of their cars, people feel comfortable with that as a true statement. But when an oil company abruptly tries to be "green sensitive" and declares its dedication to windmills and wildlife, you wonder why the company even paid the advertising team for that message. There was no hand-holding from Point A to Point D that would get the public to see that great a shift in image as logical. Would you believe the CIA if there were a sudden move to emphasize its role as a source of news for the media outlets? Of course not. You'd probably think, "That's a stretch!"

DELIBERATELY SHAPING YOUR IMAGE

- Think of every document and every public statement as a tool to manage public expectations. Keep in mind that a careless or disgruntled employee may release information never intended to go to outsiders.

- Match your public image to your audience. If your product or service is intended for people who tend to be change-averse, don't start talking about your company as unusual, fast-paced, and on the edge.

- *Image* means "persona" or "likeness"—words you use to describe people. So the person or people who publicly represent your company must be well suited for that responsibility. If you're a great CEO only for all of the "inside jobs," find someone who can do the "outside jobs."

CHAPTER TEN

The Presumption of Success

Regardless of whether your operation is recruiting an agent, making a sales call, or running a board of directors meeting, walk into the situation presuming that you will carry the day. The alternative is to assume that you will fail, or at least have discomfort about your ability to succeed. You will bleed that sense of doom.

You have a right to presume you will achieve what you want if you have forged alliances based on common interests, and you follow the rules of persuasion. And you can think of these rules in terms of both personal operations and organizational ones.

HUG YOUR ENEMY; WASH YOUR HANDS

Why do you create any alliance—on an individual or an organizational basis? An alliance enables you to do something you cannot do on your own. Whether it's hiring a particular person or forming a partnership with another company, you decide that having a working relationship provides benefits.

Henry John Temple, also known as Lord Palmerston, directed British foreign policy in the mid-nineteenth century and is credited with declaring the following in 1848, "England has no eternal friends, England has no perpetual enemies, England has only eternal and perpetual interests." From an organizational perspective, that's a good place to start to define the strategic position of a company. It's highly unlikely that your partners today will necessarily be your partners tomorrow, and even less likely that you will have the same head-to-head competitors every year. It is absolutely true that your company will have enduring interests unless you abandon your current line of business and switch industries.

During the Cold War, the Soviet Union was our adversary, even though we never came into direct conflict with one another; we did so largely through surrogates. When we fought in Vietnam, Central America, and Afghanistan, we indirectly fought the Soviet Union. From a budgetary perspective, only a small percentage of the Agency's funds for HUMINT clandestine collection operations were allocated to the Soviet Union and East Bloc countries. But a lot more than that money went to countering Soviet influences.

On June 20, 1963, a hot line was established between the Kremlin and the White House because, even though we were officially enemies, both sides recognized the value in keeping the lines of communication open so we wouldn't inadvertently destroy each other. When the Soviet Union formally dissolved, at the end of December 1991, suddenly that hot line didn't have quite the same heat. The new world order demanded that we communicate with the former countries of the Soviet Union, regarding them more like partners than as adversaries.

To that end, as intelligence officers, we tried to reach agreement with the KGB about areas of common interest. We settled on quite a few transnational problems, such as drug trafficking and organized crime. These were the areas where there could be immediate collaboration between the two intelligence services and perhaps also the two law-enforcement agencies (i.e., the FBI and its counterpart, the MVD). Analogously, the diplomats had the challenge of finding areas where they could cooperate.

The 1992 formation of Taligent, a collaboration of Apple and IBM, is one of many corporate examples of "enemies" identifying strong, common interests and letting those mutual interests set the agenda for unprecedented cooperation. In this case, Taligent had a prime mission of creating an operating system that could run on any hardware platform. The Taligent teams succeeded, laid claim to 120 U.S. patents over the next five years, and then were absorbed into IBM.

In some people's minds, the dissolution of the Soviet Union was an outright victory for the United States, and reductions in the budgets for intelligence reflected that conclusion. People were not thinking about either the interests that the United States and Russia (and other former Soviet republics) shared or the myriad new threats that resulted in the aftermath of a world where we no longer had a single "enemy." For example, the United States was concerned about Russia's nuclear devices, now sitting in remote facilities, rusting away, and vulnerable to expropriation by terrorists. So we reached out to find useful and challenging work for Russian scientists, and we joined forces with the Russians in cleaning out some of these old facilities.

The lesson from this is to get past crippling superstitions and fears so you can talk with your competitors when it makes sense. Turn them into partners if it benefits you, but be sure to keep collecting information on them. In other words, you need to spy on your allies as well as your enemies. Establishing an institutional partnership is a way of managing a portion of the relationship with a competitor—not the whole relationship, however, so you still have to be on your guard.

Sometimes getting past the dislike or distrust of people "on the other side" places a great deal of stress on the people who have to carry out the mission. One of my early contacts in the Middle East was a fellow who had been part of the leadership of a terrorist organization. They were still cohesive as a group, so it continued to be interesting to us to know what they were up to. I met with the contact occasionally to get a sense of what the group's plans were. For some people, this might have presented a moral dilemma. We had a continuing need to monitor the activities of his organization, via my contact with him, with the full knowledge that he was and continued to be a key player in the organization. His information was invaluable to us at the time and could contribute to our efforts to head off, or at least limit, the activities of the group without revealing the inside source. And we could not touch him, regardless of what he had done in the past, because at the time he was our only source of information on the group.

The complexity of the moral issue here should not escape you, no matter what you do for a living. Making deals with the devil is part and parcel of the job—something that most of us face at some point. So, sometimes the answer on how to proceed is, "What's the lesser of two evils?" Or, "If I don't do this, someone else will have to in order to achieve the goal." Or, "We have a noble mission; it's my job to help achieve it. That means doing some unpleasant things."

Usually in business the answers don't present this level of drama, but you still may be faced with having to stay close to your "enemy." In any given country, the NCS was often charged with maintaining contact with the Communist Party, particularly if it was illegal, and the other "outs." Likewise, companies may join trade associations so they can help set the lobbying agenda for their industry; if they don't show up at the table with their competitors, then it's the competitors who get to have input on legislation that may affect every company in the marketplace. And one of the reasons to go to trade shows is to stay close to the pitch and trend insights you can get from rival companies in the space.

A long time ago, one of my friends interviewed with Greenpeace, the nonprofit environmental group, in the hope of working in fund-raising. The man interviewing her told her that there were certain rules about where the money could come from; they didn't want "tainted" money. She posed the question, "What if someone wants to give us a lot of oil company stock? Would we refuse it?" Of course not, he replied. We would just sell the stock.

Another friend took an excellent consulting job with the National Rifle Association. It was a move that helped her make some good connections and learn an aspect of her business that served her well for years to come. Many of her friends took umbrage at her action, accusing her of selling out to the gun lobby. When she stuck with it and clearly seemed happy doing her work, they found a way to change their tune: They decided she was simply "repurposing" the NRA's money. (Also see the discussion of branding challenges in Chapter 9.)

As I said early in this book, the Agency needs people who have a high tolerance for ambiguity. The black-and-white world of extremists of any stripe—religious, political, philosophical—is not the world where officers of either the Agency or business organizations operate on a daily basis. We have to be diplomats, willing to hug the enemy for the sake of peace, an important deal, or a shred of intelligence.

Let's say a vendor has been supplying you exclusively with a key product ever since you opened your doors. Now you find out through your sources that the supplier has decided to supply one of your competitors, too. You're upset, because the product you'd gotten from your supplier had given you a competitive advantage. Your options are to continue with that supplier and look for a competitive advantage in another area of your business, try to find a new supplier, or confront the supplier and give him an incentive to stick with an exclusive arrangement. Your decision all depends on the value of what you're getting.

I faced this very problem with one of the agents I had handled when I was in the field early in my career. One of the station's senior assets decided to expand his options and opportunities. He was known for producing voluminous reports. In the course of reviewing his reporting, I noticed similarities between the material he reported and what we were getting from another intelligence service. The similarity triggered the question: Is he talking to them as well as us? I mounted an operation to find out how many services besides ours he might be collaborating with. All I needed to do was bug his office.

For years he had been inviting my wife and me to dinner. Typically, we tried not to mix business and pleasure, and so I had repeatedly declined. In the course of one of our routine conversations after my suspicions surfaced, I moved the discussion to a friendly tone and, once again, he issued the invitation. This time I accepted.

His residence was a kind of townhouse, with a drab exterior—identical to those around it, but opulent inside. This is typical of the region; people want to flaunt their wealth, but they do so in a way they can completely control. The living/dining area, to which he escorted my wife and me when we arrived, was upstairs, but I knew that his office was downstairs. We used to meet there, and at one meeting just before the dinner party, I'd ascertained that there was space between where the drawer of his desk closed and the end of the desk. When he left the room briefly, I had taken a quick look and figured that space would be a good spot to plant a microphone. (A perfect example of spycraft.)

The mic I brought with me to dinner that night was embedded in a foot-long wood block with batteries and a transmitter wire strapped to my leg. Fortunately, our host had invited another couple so there was a lot of getting-to-know-you chat. I had forewarned my wife that, when I excused myself from the party to go to the bathroom, she had to keep the conversation going and our host distracted. Knowing there was a bathroom downstairs, I headed down there when I excused myself. I got under his desk, lay on my back, took out the silent drill I'd slipped under my suit, drilled some holes near the back of the drawer, and installed the bug. Sawdust rained down over my chest; I collected it carefully, put it in my pocket, and rejoined the party.

After that, for a period of weeks, we monitored his conversations. Sure enough, we found him collaborating with multiple other services. And so I terminated him. (Keep in mind that this isn't a James Bond movie; by "terminate" I mean I fired him, not killed him.) I didn't tell him why, though. I just ended the relationship and moved on. Of course, we had to go through the process of identifying, vetting, and cultivating a new agent, but it was worth it to secure a loyal supplier of information.

As I have mentioned, the business of intelligence is to get information that meets certain requirements, and if that means dealing with the devil to get it, well, so be it. If the agent had been giving us critical information, we might not have dropped him, regardless of his triple dipping. It wasn't that valuable, and whatever value it did have was diminished by the fact that multiple competing organizations had it, too.

Of course, there are circumstances that might even drive us to say, "We know what you're doing and we will pay you more to drop your other customers." We wouldn't tell him how we knew; we'd fabricate a story that wouldn't suggest that we had mistrusted him. With a move like that we might be buying time, we might be buying loyalty, or we might be buying trouble. In the spy business, as well as in business, you have to consider all the options—but in the course of doing that, you make an exhaustive list of the possible repercussions in choosing each option.

MICE AT WORK

When you need to forge or maintain an alliance with someone like the agent whose office I bugged, you obviously can't rely on "common interests." The key to recruiting a spy is in pinpointing her motivation for cooperating with you at a given place, at a given time. CIA psychologists have examined this problem in a variety of ways, employing different assessment techniques to make judgments about a potential agent's personality, emotional state, and likely responses. They are then often able to provide case officers with insights so they know if they can get away with simply asking, "Do you want to work for the CIA?" or if they need to spend months cultivating a relationship.

One set of motivations can be summed up in the acronym MICE—money, ideology, coercion, and ego. Ascertaining that a target's circumstances make material gain attractive means that a bag of money might buy temporary loyalty. More loyalty in the form of information, action, or lack of action would mean another bag of money. In the case of the CIA's bribery of Afghan warlords, reported widely in late 2008, MICE became VICE, with the Agency buying information with Viagra instead of cash.

Ideology has both a positive spin and a negative one. The love of Poland that drove Ryszard Kuklinski to take the initiative in cooperating with the United States had a compelling negative side in his hatred for the grip the Soviet Union had on his homeland. Throughout history there are countless examples of people forging alliances with tribal or national powers they don't even respect, just to defeat an enemy they find ideologically repulsive. In his book *Chief of Station, Congo,* former senior operations officer Larry Devlin (2007) chronicles the fascinating drama in Central Africa's largest country when the primary enemy was often a moving target as far as the Congolese were concerned. When he arrived, the country had a president who seemed to be slipping toward a Communist alliance; the province known for its diamond mines felt it had the resources and "friends" to secede; and military leaders ran hot and cold with representatives of both the United States and the Soviet Union. Part of Devlin's job was figuring out if there was any ideological common ground, as well as calculating other motivating factors of leaders so he could make the U.S. agenda seem more desirable to them than the alternative.

Coercion is a profoundly negative motivator, but it can certainly work with someone who fears that not cooperating will jeopardize him or his family. Even so, psychologists suggest that coercion works only with particular personality types.

Ego was a factor in Edward Lee Howard's betrayal, which I referenced earlier. After his abrupt dismissal for using illegal drugs, his actions seemed like thumbing his nose at his former employer. At least in part, his ego drove him to want to bask in the appreciation of the KGB for using his connections to provide important information.

For business relationships, you can use MICE in dealing with competing interests, but it may have more use in forging alliances with people in your own company that you need to work with, or with your customers. Apply the MICE model to office politics and customer relations, and you have a new way of describing the manipulations that people around you use all the time. When you match motivator and individual well, you get what you want. When you miss, perhaps because you are projecting your own motivation on to the other person; if that's the case, you get either no cooperation or a backlash.

The money motivator in business—what we might also call a bribe in some form or another—probably takes one of these forms:

- *For an employee*— a pay raise, bonus, perks, a better office (or assignment, or title, etc.).

- *For a customer*—a discount, or perhaps additional features and benefits related to the product or service.

- *For a colleague*—lunch, drinks, or a gift.

Engaging someone's ideology in a business environment most likely relates to that person's desire to do a job with excellence. You get the individual to do more by focusing on his high standards, and the fact that those standards match your own. In trying to use ideology to motivate a client or customer, you would focus on quality, as in "I know you want the best and I'm going to give it to you."

People in business probably see a lot more coercion used than case officers do in the field. The threat of being fired, having responsibilities taken away, losing a shot at a big bonus, getting pulled from an account that involves interesting travel—bosses in many environments use these kinds of force to motivate employees. A classic example of how companies use the technique with customers comes from the world of finance. Especially in times like now, when financial institutions face intense scrutiny from regulators, credit card companies pass the pressure along to their customers. They pressure customers to cooperate if they ever want to use that card again to buy movie tickets or gasoline.

Motivating someone in business by stroking her ego is just as common. Why did people stand in line to buy iPhones when they first came out? Because they needed them? No, they did it because Apple did a magnificent job of convincing people they were special if they had one. Companies with an excellent track record in building brand loyalty commonly create ads with ego appeal. It is the very essence of campaigns by luxury retailers.

Delving into these motivators a little deeper, you can see how they might interplay, depending on the individual circumstances. Intelligence historian H. Keith Melton, a recognized expert in clandestine devices and technology who serves on our board of directors at the International Spy Museum, describes the most significant indicators of why they work in a recruitment situation:

> CIA psychologists found three of the most significant indicators of a willingness to spy were split loyalties (potentially evidenced by extramarital affairs or intense dislike of a supervisor), narcissism (when seen as excessively self-absorbed, arrogant, and vain), and dissidence in parental relationship. Added to these were contributing circumstances such as failed

careers, marriage problems, infidelity, and substance abuse. Seldom was there a single motivating factor, and most recruitments were based upon a combination of vulnerabilities. . . . . CIA psychologists concluded that for most agents the susceptibility to recruitment and the willingness to act is the highest between ages of thirty-five and forty-five, a time of personal reevaluation and mid-life crisis commonly experienced in many cultures. (Wallace and Melton, 2008, p. 365)

Keith exposes a few transferable points in this analysis. The first emerges from the fact that all of these conditions underlying vulnerabilities run across humanity. You are as likely to see self-absorbed and emotionally conflicted people at a business meeting as you are in an Agency recruiting encounter. You will definitely see middle-aged people in transition as family, financial, and perhaps health problems start to occupy a more prominent part of their lives. At some point, you will probably be one of these people, if you aren't already.

A few ways you can use these motivational insights are:

* *Do a self-evaluation exercise.* Are you distracted or conflicted to an extent that you're vulnerable to the persuasive abilities of people around you, or in a way that diminishes your effectiveness at work? You may not want to stop having an affair, and you certainly can't do a thing about the fact that your daughter is turning eighteen and is about to leave for college, but you can recognize that these situations can weaken you as a professional.

* *Pay attention to your colleagues; help them if they show signs of those vulnerabilities.* Someone who disrupts a meeting with a rude remark or doesn't complete a project on time may be using bad behavior as a cry for help. A very good friend of mine worked in a small company of about forty people. The office manager, one of the new CEO's first hires, was a tyrant, but made a supreme effort to please the boss. He would thank her by writing "well done!" on Post-it notes, which she placed all over the walls of her office. Word got around about

Judy and her Post-it notes. The joke faded quickly, but a few caring people realized she obviously had some unmet emotional needs, and they started deliberately being nicer to her. The turn-around in her attitude and behavior wasn't immediate, but it did happen.

- *Use your perception to connect more strongly with a customer or client.* I'm not suggesting you prey on the fact that you've picked up that a person has problems. But you can serve that person and your company well by listening and being empathetic. The mechanics of establishing a connection in this manner are covered in the next section of this chapter, on the stages of persuasion. In brief, it starts with being aware that something isn't normal. A former colleague saw that his consulting client was distracted, so he moved from shop talk to inquire casually about the man's family. The client admitted that his son, a successful high school wrestler, had been caught using steroids and the ensuing health and legal concerns pulled his attention off work. The admission invited a confidential response— a quid pro quo—and, once received, they were able to move back to the work issues at hand.

THE PATH OF PERSUASION

As I mentioned earlier, there are only a handful of categories into which all jobs fit, and most of the time there is some kind of cross-pollination. So you may think of yourself as a CEO or an accountant, but there are times when you are a persuader, just like a sales professional or a case officer. And so the skills and insights covered in this section apply to you as well.

Analogously, organizations follow a path of persuasion. Implicit in any "About us" paragraph or mission statement is an invitation to participate, to buy into, to vote—to do something so that the mission can be accomplished. The American Red Cross, for example, says "The American Red Cross is where people mobilize to help their neighbors." This is a feat that cannot be done unless they convince people to turn to them to mobilize.

The Path for an Individual

A CEO will go right through the stages of persuasion in a sales presentation in a board or staff meeting. She will make a connection with the people in the room, build a trust bond, ask the right questions to find out what they need to know to take the next step, make a presentation that incorporates answers to those questions, invite and overcome objections, and then close the deal.

The descriptions that John Naples, senior training consultant for Encore Consulting Group, gives to the stages of a sales presentation correspond with those I might use to talk about how case officers recruit agents and engage assets. They make sense in describing any persuasive encounter. You will notice that the elicitation techniques, importance of understanding body language, and ability to perceive someone's emotional state—all of which I discussed in Chapter 5—come into play here.

Stage 1: Forming the Trust Bond Effective selling is a process that starts with establishing a rapport and a trust bond that is rooted in your credibility. That allows you to persuade someone to listen, to buy, to do what you ask.

Although the names for the process are different in the sales arena and in recruiting agents, the interplay of intuition and judgment are the same. It's what John calls *aligning*—that is, trying to get on the same wavelength as the individual so you have a reliable reading of his thinking and emotions.

The body language associated with this is called mirroring. As John instructs his clients in sales training, "You pace yourself, your physiology reflects the other person's, and your tonal quality and volume of voice move in the direction of theirs to cultivate a sense of trust." For anyone who has studied neurolinguistic programming (NLP), this advice has a very familiar ring.

I want to draw a distinction here between the recommendation to incorporate elements of another person's behavior into your presentation and that of impersonating him. In a really great performance, like Philip Seymour Hoffman's portrayal of Truman Capote in the film *Capote*, you have a sense of how Capote thought and felt. In contrast to capturing a character in the way Hoffman did, an impersonation gives a superficial look at how the person expresses thoughts and feelings. In other words, whether you're selling a computer system or recruiting an agent, you don't want to be one of the comics on *Saturday Night Live* doing an imitation of a politician. You want to be you, using mirroring to connect with another person mentally, as well as physically.

When you have an intense, driven person you're mirroring, get right down to business. You will win her over a lot more easily than trying to chat about the weather. In contrast, Maryann once had a meeting with the CEO of a company who took casual Friday to extremes—he was in shorts and stocking feet. He wanted to begin the meeting by talking about his run at lunchtime. She figured the best way to make a connection with him was to reference her own run before breakfast. To some people, that would seem like a waste of time, but to someone who feels that a fellow jock is someone who speaks his language, it's the starting point for a trust bond.

Stage 2: Making Discoveries This is the time to probe. You ask pointed questions to identify the person's concerns, challenges, needs, wants. John Naples calls them *HOT questions*: high yield, open-ended, and thought provoking. The answers help you discern what potential lies in the particular situation and you get the customer, or whoever is your audience, thinking about the nature and benefits of a relationship with you.

The questions you ask reveal opportunities. It's like any game in which you set up a shot or position yourself to score. You tell me what I need to know so that I have leverage over you. John puts a lot of emphasis on how this is not a self-serving exercise: "The session is all about them—about their functional and emotional needs."

You need to identify the other person's emotional agenda and then pull the heart strings by expressing how you can deliver on that agenda. A recruitment in which ideology is a motivator might well involve emotion that the case officer could cultivate. When Ryszard Kuklinski met with his handler, he walked in with faith that collaborating with the United States would help him serve his motherland. His hatred of the Soviet domination of Poland shaped a powerful emotional agenda that enabled him to risk a great deal to work with us.

You have to have conviction that what you offer is great, too. When you believe that what you have to offer will improve someone else's life, then you can engage people in a genuine way. You deserve their trust.

Stage 3: Delivering the Presentation Whatever you say has to have veracity and strength. That comes not only from having your facts straight and believing in your product or service but also from your ability to address the person's needs squarely. You have to demonstrate that you actually paid attention to the answers to the *HOT questions*. That requires an attention to detail that can be difficult for people who fancy themselves only big-picture thinkers. Keep in mind that superior and consistently successful chief executives have a command of vital details that keeps everyone, from the board of directors to office assistants, in awe of them.

Stage 4: Either Addressing Objections or Closing At this point, one of two things will happen: the client will either raise an objection, which you can then address; or you can go straight to closing. For the latter, you begin the closing with a simple trial question, such as "What do you think?" Or, "Does this line up with your objective?" That gives you feedback and, you hope, an opening. The person will say, "I'm a little curious about this" or "What's next?"

The close is just an invitation to take the next step: asking him to take action. The close should never be hard and direct, as if you're trying to slam someone verbally against the wall. It's more like "Would you like to dance?" than it is "And now we're going to waltz!"

In the sales environment, just as in the recruiting environment, objections are good. They open the door, allowing you to address concerns and advance the relationship. In fact, the worst thing that can happen is having an objection go unstated. If someone thinks the price of doing business with you is too high, show some empathy, rather than going on the attack.

If I were trying to recruit someone with a family, and he thought that cooperating with me could jeopardize his children, I could not move forward until I acknowledged that I respect his concern for his family. And I'd be wise to back it up with some explanation, just as a sales professional might say to someone who is price sensitive, "I've had other clients express similar concerns, and here's what I did . . . ."

Asking for permission to address the objection shows respect, too. It can also effect a slight power shift that is beneficial in continuing to build trust. "May I take a minute and tackle that?" is one way of lowering the level of control that you might appear to have. You're not defensive. You're not offensive. You're there to provide answers and opportunities, to lay out the value proposition.

* * *

Social intelligence, aka charisma, is integral to success throughout this process. It's the ability to read people, read situations, and then adapt according to what you learn. You have to absorb relevant information so you know how to act and what to say.

The Path for an Organization

Organizations can see the stages of persuasion as a guide to reinforcing their position in the marketplace.

Stage 1: Forming the Trust Bond The most dramatic way to see the importance of stage 1 is to see what happens when a company loses its rapport and corrupts its trust bond with the public. AIG stands out in this crowd, but a lot of other companies have suffered periodic setbacks because of unfulfilled promises, misleading statements, or even deaths. Many years ago, Ford lost ground when the public learned that the gas tanks on Pintos exploded in rear-end collisions, owing to a design flaw that company executives were aware of prior to release of the car. Shareholders, as well as women taking the contraceptive Yaz, got angry at Bayer when the Food and Drug Administration determined that the company had no grounds to promote the contraceptive as an acne treatment, among other angles. And then there are the countless stories on the Internet of restaurants losing patrons when they discover substitutions of pork for veal or cod for haddock. There's obviously nothing wrong with pork or cod, but the misrepresentation makes people suspicious of what else might not be what it seems to be.

News releases, ads, and public statements must project trustworthiness and credibility, and they must be backed up with actions that reinforce those attributes. Throughout the years, the Agency's public track record in this area has been uneven, so this is one lesson learned that may be as much rooted in failure as it is in success.

The concept of organizational mirroring presents lots of interesting cases of both success and failure, depending on how the mirroring is done. The successes tend to come from a company's paying attention to the characteristics and preferences of customers and mirroring them. The failures come from a company's "seeing itself" in its target audience—even though those people look and act nothing like what the company thinks they do.

Although they've hit a few bumps in the road, BMW has traditionally done a good job of "selling to its own"—that is, of focusing on people who already own BMWs and engendering continued loyalty by delivering on expectations of that demographic. The expectations of image relate to the car, showroom, literature, and even what movies have a character driving a BMW. The expectations of service reflect the fact that BMW owners have lots of demands on them; they want "peace of mind" with a vehicle, which is what BMW says it offers with its service package. In fact, many companies with high-end products know that they must mirror the lifestyle and taste of their clientele in terms of product placement, ads, appearance of the store, and so on. Would someone buy a Rolex from a vendor on the sidewalk, even if the watch were the real thing? Chances are good that the person who can afford a real Rolex would walk right past the "opportunity" because in his mind the presentation conflicts with where that kind of product belongs.

One of the winners in the contest for "seeing what you want to see in the mirror" is the United States. We can use military historian Roberta Wohlstetter's (1962) term "failure of imagination" to describe why we did not consider that Japan might bomb Pearl Harbor; but another way of describing the failure is that, to some extent, we saw ourselves when we looked at the enemy. We did the same thing at the onset of the Cuban Missile Crisis; an attack by Nikita Khrushchev simply didn't make sense to the American mind—what could possibly be gained?

When Apple Computer introduced the Newton, the first so-called personal digital assistant, the engineering and marketing teams (at least one of whom has "evangelist" on his business card) envisioned hordes of people eagerly adopting a technology that allowed them to write instead of having to type. Their failure of imagination was that they had too much imagination. They saw doctors writing prescriptions at a patient's bedside and the order being wirelessly transmitted to the pharmacy on the first floor. They saw executives scribbling memos that instantly became readable text to their staff. They looked in the mirror and saw people who thought Newton was cool, just like they did. It turned out to be more a hallucination than a view of realistic possibilities. As we all know, it did not take Apple too long to get the vision right.

Stage 2: Making Discoveries An organization does not have to ask any questions to be good at the discovery phase, but it does have to have mechanisms for receiving and responding to input. I have a friend who bought a contact lens solution labeled "TSA-approved," but the bottle was apparently .6 ounces larger than the Transportation Security Administration actually allowed for carry-on luggage. She called the company about the confiscation, and within five minutes had gotten an apology for the inconvenience, made arrangements to replace the product, and received a thank-you for helping them correct the error. Since they had her on the phone, they obtained a little more information so they could send a package with the replacement item that contained coupons for other items she commonly bought from the company. The process, then, was not one of "probe and then listen," as John Naples described in the sales cycle; it was "listen and then probe." The result was the same, in that the seller learned something important about the customer that could be used to reinforce the relationship.

Organizations that are inept at the discovery stage have Web sites with feedback forms but no options to engage on live chats or obtain phone numbers; and they do not give customer service people any decision-making authority—not one bit of discretion—in addressing problems. That's because the process of discovery has an instant-gratification aspect to it; it's about having an exchange that opens the door to opportunities for the seller. If the door opens and the customer feels nothing but cold air, the company has failed at stage 2. The emotional engagement may occur, but it's in the form of revulsion.

A type of stage 2 test for the Agency occurs during the opportunity to answer questions from Congress. Trust rises or falls (as may the Agency's budget) depending on how well the person testifying satisfies the functional and emotional needs of the committee.

Stage 3: Delivering the Presentation In the old days—say, the early 2000s—a company "presentation" to its customers or clients was most likely a one-way street. Advertising and marketing materials took what the company learned in the discovery phase and packaged it. The presentation itself is now becoming interactive, with companies like Procter & Gamble setting up social-networking sites to make the presentation personal. The aim is to stop talking at consumers and to start talking with them.

Stage 4: Either Addressing Objections or Closing All eyes are on a company like Johnson & Johnson when people die as a result of ingesting one of their products. J&J executives were both honorable and practical in their response when that happened with their drug Tylenol, despite the fact that it was clear from the beginning that the problem was almost certainly not "their fault." They distributed warnings nationwide, ran public-service announcements to prevent people from taking Tylenol, stopped producing the painkiller, and pulled ads. They also promptly issued a recall of the estimated 31 million bottles of all Tylenol products in circulation—and that alone meant $100 million to the company. Later on, after a final determination had been made that the cause was someone's tampering with Tylenol capsules, J&J offered to exchange the capsules already purchased with tablets.

As a result of their actions, many of us who have since been in the spotlight as public affairs officers for a government agency or public relations directors for a company have learned from J&J's PR success. They faced the ultimate objection—your product causes death—and met it head on with intelligence that probably secured them more brand loyalty than they could buy through advertising.

This returns to the issue of the trust bond. Whether you're meeting an objection or going for the close, trust must strengthen, not diminish.

USING PROJECTION

People see what they want to see and believe what they want to believe. It's called projection, and it is a manifestation of trust, to some extent. This is the flaw in a lot of marketing "data." The people collecting the data have an agenda they want to support, and so they find the information that supports it, inadvertently or even deliberately ignoring the salient facts.

As a Clandestine officer, I tend to be skeptical. Most people do not cultivate healthy skepticism, however, and many flawed products have still had success among consumers because human beings are basically trusting. Think snake oil.

A friend of mine who does media consulting with a lot of high-technology companies got a contract in the mid-1990s to set up a media tour related to the beta version of a product that would be launched in a few months. Her job was to set up East Coast and West Coast editorial briefings for the company CEO. The product was a small, ruggedized computer designed for special applications of particular interest to law enforcement, manufacturing, and other groups requiring something light, strong, able to use cellular signals, and with the ability to do handwriting recognition, among other special features.

My friend created a package of briefing materials describing the functionality of the product, as described to her. She was genuinely excited and pitched the product so well that nearly all of the editors she contacted invited a briefing.

Success: A full schedule for the CEO.

Failure—potentially: The product didn't work exactly the way it was supposed to work. When the time came for the briefings, the product was more of an alpha-plus, rather than a beta. She didn't know that until the first briefing.

The CEO was no dummy. Having had about twenty years' experience at that point with state-of-the-art technology, he realized the value of smoke and mirrors. He would hold the computer with his large hand on the back panel when introducing it to editors. He needed a large hand because the back of the computer was falling off. He would then turn the device around and use his free hand to point out the unique slots on the back of the computer that gave it extraordinary functionality—or what was extraordinary at the time.

In nearly twenty briefings, no one ever asked him to drop it to test the ruggedized feature. No one ever said, "Could I play with it?" My friend told me, "We got 100 percent fabulous reviews on something that no one even touched."

DESERVING YOUR PRESUMED SUCCESS

- In forming alliances, define your common interests up front.

- When you do not have common interests, be sure you specify how the alliance can help you meet your own requirements.

- Pinpoint the motivation(s) for an "antagonist" to cooperate with you—remember MICE.

- Keep the states of selling in mind as you interact with a prospect: form a trust bond, make discoveries, deliver your presentation that reflects discoveries, and address objections/close.

- When you present to your prospect, know that people see what they want to see to a great extent. Make that projection work for you, not against you.

• •

CHAPTER ELEVEN

Meeting Change with Intelligence

In this chapter, the concept of "shifting sands" underlies a focus on outcome thinking and normalizing change.

OUTCOME THINKING
• •

In my view, *outcome thinking* is what some people call contingency planning, but with an added component. Outcome thinking implies a readiness to change the goal itself, not just the method of achieving a goal. It is a predictive exercise to determine the implications down the road and how to sequence actions so as to get the best result, not just the predetermined one.

When President John F. Kennedy asked the nation to "commit itself to achieving the goal, before this decade is out, of landing a man on the moon and returning him safely to the Earth," his strategic vision was so specific that scientists and engineers really had no wiggle room to change the goal. Sometimes, that's the nature of the situation, in which case your best approach is to go thorough contingency planning. When an agent misses a scheduled rendezvous or fails to follow through on a dead drop, we don't know what happened: did he not navigate well, was he sick, or did he fear someone had him under surveillance? We rethink the operation as we look for "signs of life" indications, which have been prearranged. It may be something like carrying a red box into a post office on the second Tuesday of the month. Our goal may have been to get him out of the country within a month; based on what we learn after reconnecting, we may have to get his whole family out of the country in a week.

Two Types of Thinking

Outcome thinking has two varieties: linear and branching. *Linear* describes the kind of regulated "if, then" sequence of enabling events that you find in a recipe: chop, sauté, add seasoning, bake, and you get the dish. If logic tells you that *A* leads to *B* and *B* leads to *C*, then your challenge is simply to make sure you have considered all of the letters of the alphabet in the correct sequence. Dell's decision to offer its own brand of printer rather than have an ongoing arrangement with Hewlett-Packard was a tactical departure that provoked changes in relationships with vendors, customers, and a strategic partner. They carried it off, which would suggest a good sense of how one action affects a subsequent one. *Branching* describes what physicians go through in determining how to treat a patient with a complicated illness or with multiple serious injuries. They try to ascertain how to set a chain of events in motion that will lead to the best outcome, given that multiple paths are possible after the first action is taken.

One of my favorite stories about outcome thinking in the intelligence arena comes from World War II. It demonstrates the planning and predictive ability people had about achieving something that many heads of state and military leaders would have labeled impossible. They could see that if they could put a certain plan in motion, then they would win a key battle on the road to winning the war. At the same time, if their stratagem didn't work as predicted, options on actions down the road were still there.

On April 30, 1943, the Royal Navy prepared a corpse carefully to look like a British officer and placed the body to float at sea toward the Spanish coast, with a briefcase attached to him. When the body drifted to the shore, Spain's military claimed it and thought they had found vital intelligence information. Inside the briefcase were Allied plans for troop movements—and those plans did not include Sicily. After sharing the contents with the Germans, to whom they were sympathetic, the Spanish returned the body to the Brits, reassuring them that they did not disturb anything in the briefcase. By that time, the contents were known in Berlin and Hitler responded accordingly. He moved Nazi troops to Greece, Sardinia, and Corsica. This ruse, which was the brainchild of a British naval intelligence lawyer named Ewen Montagu, helped set the stage for a successful Allied invasion of Sicily that led to the fall of Benito Mussolini and, ultimately, to the surrender of Italy to the Allies on September 3, 1943.

There are probably contemporary examples of this kind of deception, but as you may suspect, this is the kind of material that remains classified for quite some time. The business world is not without its own tales of decoys and gambits that reflect outcome thinking. In his book *Crossing Fifth Avenue to Bergdorf Goodman*, former Bergdorf CEO Ira Neimark (2007) tells the story of the store's "Italian Strategy." In part, it involved sneaking out of a fashion show featuring a top French designer to meet secretly with an Italian designer, and then surreptitiously flying to Rome. Neimark says, "I had to use every trick Ian Fleming had ever taught me in order to slip unseen into Charles De Gaulle Airport. Everything felt distinctly cloak-and-dagger" as he dodged other merchants, as well as the head of *Women's Wear Daily*, in pursuit of his "Italian connection." The strategy of securing an exclusive with Fendi guided his moves because securing that arrangement meant that other top Italian designers would soon follow suit. And they did. Had Fendi decided not to cooperate, he could have still executed the plan by wooing another top house first.

The Bay of Pigs is one high-profile example of a lack of outcome thinking. The planning for the operation seemed sound; the case officers involved knew their mission. But part of the planning process has to be an honest evaluation of resources over which you have control. If you're going to set your sights on a goal that cannot be changed as new intelligence arrives, then you had better know exactly who and what can be brought in to aid the effort at every step of the way. Unfortunately, air support was a critical part of the invasion plan, and President Kennedy did not authorize it. As former DCI Richard Helms admitted in a 1981 interview recorded by Ralph E. Weber in *Spymasters: Ten CIA Officers in Their Own Words* (2002), that disaster helped reform Agency thinking: "The Bay of Pigs taught everyone, whether they were involved directly or indirectly, a lesson . . . that an organization like the CIA should not undertake such a mission, because they don't have the general staff system and the support mechanisms to underpin an activity of that kind and of that size involving that much support equipment, such as boats, airplanes, training camps, and all of the rest of it."

SORTING THE INFLUENCES

Who or what has primary influence on the way you devise your plan of action and identify your contingencies? As I've mentioned, the mentoring process in the Agency gives case officers the benefit of senior officers' wisdom and experience. Combine that with rigorous training in hard and soft skills, and you should come up with a good knowledge base for outcome thinking. But then for many people, the stories can kick in—the things we may have read in the *Studies in Intelligence* journal and the books by colleagues and investigative journalists. And so, part of the challenge becomes sorting the influences.

For some people, the strongest influences on their plans and tactics would be a creed or a set of rules. The Ranger Creed lays out six precepts— each one beginning with a letter in the word *Ranger*—that are meant to guide Army Rangers in that process. They know it by heart, so staying close to the precepts is ingrained behavior. In business, some people rely on guidelines like Al Ries and Jack Trout's *22 Immutable Laws of Marketing*. If that's your source of business wisdom, then you believe that, "It is better to be first than it is to be better." But if you choose to adopt outcome thinking, you will find occasions to reject this law. Outcome thinking involves assigning weight to real-time, situation-specific judgments and not just relying on a principle that worked in the past or seems logical. In this case, my experience in the field would dictate a rewrite in most circumstances as, "It is better to be the most valued than it is to be first."

Consider the circumstance of trying to recruit an agent in Iraq. You want his loyalty to be to you, and so you do what it takes to get him to perceive a relationship with you as much more valuable than with anyone else. It could involve money, emigration assistance, and other material inducements, as well as a compelling ideological argument; part of your job is to determine what the person values most. It's the same thing if you try to "recruit" a new customer who bought a product from the company that was first to market with it. If you come in with a competing product that gives that customer higher margins in his business, or an advantage in the marketplace, then you have a better argument than, "I was here first."

NORMALIZING CHANGE

Using outcome thinking requires a certain amount of emotional agility, as well as mental dexterity. You may be capable of changing tactics or a goal based on new intelligence, but that would take many people off their game. And not only will you have the change-averse resisting a new direction, you may also have institutional memory working against you. It's the "We've always done it this way" mind-set, the natural inclination to revert to the known and familiar. As part of the normal course of business, therefore, you might put certain elements into place to make it easier to effect change when necessary, whether it's a planned exercise or an unexpected one.

In the CIA, the equivalent of a branch office is the field station, but each field station can't afford to focus solely on its business in a particular country. It has to connect to the overarching mission by staying aware of what other stations are doing, to whatever extent possible. It's not just a matter of focusing on the mission; it's a practical matter in terms of operations. Just because one station's officers are sitting in a relatively calm environment, in a friendly European country, doesn't mean they won't be collecting intelligence on myriad other topics that have nothing to do with the country itself.

This is the reality that helps the case officer respond efficiently to both planned and unanticipated changes in the requirements that guide his activities. The Agency cannot afford to send new requirements to the field, only to have case officers go through an emotional cycle analogous to the grief cycle described by Elizabeth Kübler Ross in her book *On Death and Dying.* You can't produce well if you're experiencing denial and anger when you first hear about a big change and you end up at acceptance only after going through a bout of depression.

Planned Change

The "grief cycle" among employees is a reality for executives who introduce change but do nothing to normalize it. A change in leadership from an easygoing CEO to a hard-charger, or going public with the company, or changing the benefits package—these are all examples of planned changes that a company has no excuse for handling badly in terms of preparing its employees.

Any organization facing a planned change can take a lesson from the less-than-stellar way that the Department of Defense handled the mandate of "black berets for all," made in October 2000. When U.S. Army Chief of Staff General Eric Shinseki and Deputy Defense Secretary Paul Wolfowitz announced that black berets would be standard issue for soldiers, the Army Rangers respectfully rebelled. For decades, the black beret had symbolized their status as an elite corps; in fact, they often referred to it as the "coveted Black Beret" and capitalized the first letters. They argued that issuing black berets to every soldier was a meaningless change in terms of what the brass intended it to accomplish—that is, symbolize the transformation of the Army as a whole.

The military has the power to mandate change. Nevertheless—after the fact—the Army chose to try to normalize the change and worked out a compromise: black berets would be standard issue, but Rangers would receive tan berets as a sign of distinction rooted in the tradition of Rogers' Rangers, the legendary colonial unit that inspired the modern Rangers, and the buckskin hats they wore. Not a perfect solution as far as many Rangers were concerned, but it did mitigate resistance.

Contrast this with the way Jack Welch, former Chairman and CEO of General Electric, followed through on his commitment to involve every employee in radical change through his Work-Out program, modeled after town meetings. Welch wanted nothing shy of a corporate revolution that included inviting employees to make suggestions directly to their bosses and, whenever possible, getting immediate feedback. The quantifiable result was taking the company from a market capitalization of about $12 billion when he assumed leadership in 1981 to a market cap of more than $500 billion when he left twenty years later.

Unexpected Change

Unlike the black beret and GE situations, there are shifts that catch everyone off-guard. If you have the mentoring in place, as well as the strategic leadership, then theoretically you should be able to move people toward that unexpected change quickly—more so than in organizations where there is less focus on connections among members of the team.

The first thing you do when handling unexpected change is tell people why the change is happening now. Remove all doubt that the boss is Chicken Little, yelling that everyone has to scatter in new directions because the sky is falling. The second thing you do is remind people why they can handle it. The Agency does an excellent job of reminding case officers that they have the skills to do their job well. When requirements change, the message is something like, "You've proven yourself. All we're asking you to do is do it differently." The third thing to do when handling unexpected change is to move people toward fulfilling the new requirement, with a strong sense of the mission-related reward that follows.

The process of managing the change can get undermined, and the distinction between planned and unplanned change can be blurred when politics overtake logic, unfortunately. For example, in national politics, the question might be "Is there true urgency behind this regulatory crackdown, or is it a political tactic?" While the examples are often dramatic with national politics, it's a daily occurrence with companies where office politics are a thriving influence.

Let's say that, in the aftermath of a bad quarter and a formal damage assessment, a company CEO decides that the organization needs a new course of action to increase its margins. The marketing group collects solid marketing data that indicate that the sales team has been focusing on the wrong market and emphasizing the wrong product. The recommendations from the marketing group challenge some core values of the company: the salesperson controls his own customer base and that salesperson's front-line knowledge of customer needs supersedes other input, so you have internal strife. This is how the organization does this particular thing, and it should continue that way because "it's not broken."

Conflicting views like this create problems related to personal behavior, organizational structure, and strategic leadership. The CEO and other senior executives can revamp the structure, keep people informed of changes, implement incentives to change, and emphasize the likely rewards of implementing a new model—but they can't alter the personalities involved. Some people may still be unhappy with their marching orders and end up engendering dysfunction in their team.

Countering Dysfunction in a Team

Two ways to downplay or eliminate disruptive influences on a team are spotlighting the differences among people and implementing a structure to direct the flow of work and constrain objections. As I mentioned earlier, case officers tend to have no trouble vocalizing opinions, so we generally get a good idea of how people are different in basic ways—word choices, in organizing their thoughts, and so on. And the sense of urgency often associated with our Agency work tends to keep it moving forward.

In my experience with companies, I have seen how a conscious effort to use those two actions can help teams get past crippling disharmony. One such disabled group was composed of technology professionals from different companies. Their agenda involved managing the development of standards for certain types of computer hardware. In frustration over the fact that delegates to the organization weren't even polite to each other sometimes, the group's new leader brought in a consultant who began his presentation to the thirty people sitting in a large rectangular configuration with, "Lids down, please." Everyone understood precisely what he meant.

In an almost metronomic rhythm, as people followed one another, the lids of their laptops—their barriers so they wouldn't have to look at each other—went down. He then went to a flip chart and wrote one word: *bow*. And then he looked around while he pointed to the word and asked, "What does this mean?" One by one, they shouted answers. "Something you wear in your hair." "What you do when you meet someone important." "A gesture at a curtain call." "The thing on my shoes." And, finally, the last contribution from a pet lover: "Half a dog's hello." It was a simple exercise, but it introduced the point that they then explored in more work-specific ways. They discussed how their point of view, vocabulary, and academic backgrounds affected the way they worked, or didn't work, together—even more so than the fact they worked for competing companies.

As the newly selected head, the leader also had an opening to make some procedural upgrades. She used the rules established for standards development by the American National Standards Institute with precision and consistency. They were set up to channel the flow of the work, put limits on what kind of objections could be entered, and enforce time limits on how long objections could hold up progress. The group had its problems, largely associated with the personalities at the table, but they still managed to get a lot of work done.

MONITORING RESPONSES TO PRESSURE

Sometimes individuals become dysfunctional, disrupting the workflow of entire groups, because of how they respond to pressure. I devoted a lot of words up front to recruiting top performers and the means by which you can keep them engaged, but as part of the discussion of improving your organization, you need to consider how intense demands can affect the ability of people to function—even seasoned professionals.

Covert operations are risky by nature; Clandestine officers are paid to take risks. Any operation has the potential to fail, and the consequences range from not succeeding in getting a little piece of information to rupturing relations with another country to losing a life. The span of consequences that can occur is broad. So, doing something covertly raises the bar in terms of consequences. If you do something openly, then everyone sees what you're doing and can offer insights along the way and help you debrief if you fail. With a covert operation, the contributing factors to failure may be as secret as the operation itself.

In addition to those demands of risk and secrecy, case officers also know well the tyranny of urgency. For our work to have any value, the information we produce must be timely. At a senior staff meeting, someone asked the Director of Central Intelligence, Admiral Turner, "What is our most important resource?" He said, "People." His deputy, Frank Carlucci (who later became secretary of defense), said, "No, Stan. It's time." If intelligence is not timely, it's no good.

What we have learned over the course of years, and sometimes the hard way, is that case officers may be exceptional people in many ways, but they are still people. The relentless pressures to perform can exacerbate health or relationship problems. We have learned that addressing the impact of that pressure directly and working with the individual goes a long way toward improving the organization. Any HR professional would probably say, "Well, that's obvious." The subtle lesson, though, is that different people can define "relentless pressure" in very different ways.

When case officers go into the field, they have been prepared to whatever extent possible to deal with the risk and secrecy. The impact of time as it relates to the work is known, but harder to describe. For instance, the word *vacation* nearly drops out of their vocabulary. When I was with the Agency, we held the government record for the highest rate of leave hours not used. And the big joke in the field was, "How do you spot the people at U.S. installations who are actually intelligence officers?" Their cars are the ones in the parking lot on Saturday.

For that reason, there are burnouts in the intelligence business, especially during a time of crisis, when the pressure to deliver remains relentless. The Agency has people and programs to help them—as you probably do—but they don't make the situation go away. One preventative measure that may help is to add a category to your performance evaluation form—not a category for judging, but for understanding. In conversation, try to figure out how much pressure the employee perceives at the moment. Is it like that all the time? Is it necessary or artificial? Answers to questions like these could go a long way toward preventing problems for that person and improving your organizational performance.

SUPPORTING INDIVIDUAL AND ORGANIZATION AGILITY

- Determine whether your goal is etched in stone or could and should change based on new intelligence.

- Analyze your sequence of planned actions in two ways: as if it were a recipe (must do X before Y) and as if it were standing dominoes (one event will force the next). Use that to help you determine alternative courses of action.

- It's normal for change to evoke an emotional response— a version of the "grief cycle"—so give people reasons for change and early alerts about it when possible.

- Embed in your organization certain elements that help people respond well to unanticipated change: a method and style of communicating new marching orders; mentoring so people know whom to trust and go to throughout a transition; mission clarity.

- Address team dysfunction by spotlighting differences among team members, so at least they understand why they aren't getting along, and putting a structure in place to keep them moving in the same direction.

- Periodically try to ascertain how much pressure employees feel they're under. You aren't doing it to judge, but rather to understand what may be affecting a person's ability to function.

CHAPTER TWELVE

Damage Assessment

One major case that has negatively affected the CIA in the last quarter-century is the treason of Aldrich Ames. "Rick" Ames began spying in 1985 and was arrested by the FBI in February 1994. The effect of this mole's actions has rippled through the agency and the U.S. government. The body count attributed to his betrayal includes Major General Dmitri Polyakov, then the highest-ranking official in the Russian military intelligence group GRU, who was providing intelligence to the United States during the 1980s. The Soviets executed him in 1988, after Rick Ames exposed him.

Anyone who worked with Ames after he turned would have to wonder: Did I ever see anything that, in retrospect, seemed questionable? Certainly before he turned, all of us who had exposure to him did not see anything out of the ordinary.

In doing a damage assessment in a case like Rick Ames's, such questions about what people saw that might make sense in retrospect are part of a reverse-engineering process to determine how much the person exposed and injured operations. In this case, Ames gave up a certain amount of information that we could identify. The question remained, "What did he give that we didn't know about?" And the question that precedes that one is, "What did he actually know?" Working backward, we can try to figure out the maximum potential damage, assuming he gave up everything he knew.

It's hard to get people to cooperate fully in a damage assessment like this one because getting the whole picture means involving people who have been betrayed. They are feeling guilty about promoting him, vulnerable about having had candid conversations with him—and yet you are asking them to come clean about every debate, memo, and watercooler chat they ever had with the person. And it's not just a matter of what cases had been compromised. It's a matter of determining what flaws in the system allowed this to happen.

Bernard Madoff is Wall Street's equivalent of Aldrich Ames, a betrayer of trust at the expense of other people's lives and fortunes. The damage assessment of his Ponzi scheme also involves a "what" and a "how": What is the full extent of the damage, and how did he get away with it? Assessing the full extent of the damage requires an army of number crunchers. Not only is there the ripple effect of investors' losses but also there is the confusion over whose money went where, since Madoff's sources included feeder funds with clients who thought their money was being managed by one firm, when it was actually in Madoff's hands. And as part of the ripple effect, investigators will confront some life-and-death questions, just as Ames's investigators did. In this case, it's everything from medical-care issues related to a Parkinson's sufferer who lost her money because of Madoff, to the Ethiopian Jews and Darfuri refugees who the swindled Eli Weisel Foundation were assisting. And as with Ames, the "how" involves an enormous number of people because he got away with it for so long. From Madoff's own family members to the heads of the feeder funds to SEC regulators—who knows something that could explain how this travesty could be sustained for so long?

THE OVERSIGHT FUNCTION

Businesses often have internal oversight, but it may not be organization-wide. For example, the quality-control experts in engineering may serve that oversight function for engineering, and human resources may do it generally for personnel matters. For the CIA, the inspector general—the Agency's chief internal overseer—has responsibility for Agency-wide oversight. The range of responsibilities includes:

- Financial auditing, just like any company

- Wrongdoing, which involves investigation into bad behavior; again, companies tend to have this as part of the HR function

- Management auditing, which focuses on operations glitches with the purpose of improving practices and processes

When I was with the Inspector General's (IG) office, I was part of the team performing management audits. We would take a team into the field and look into every facet of operations and administration. First, we'd read in, just as an officer being sent to the field for the first time would. Next, we would talk with everyone at CIA headquarters and at the facility who had personal knowledge of the operations there. Then we'd do a report.

So far, this should sound remarkably like the process that consultants follow in doing management audits. But then the process likely diverges from those of many corporate consulting firms. We would talk with the principal people interfacing with our field element. For example, let's say I'm talking with a major agency facility in San Francisco and they regularly deal with the FBI and a military office in the area. We would interview those people and then come back to Headquarters and interview the main customers of that facility.

We can then answer questions about the unit's operations and productivity that few companies could get from an analogous process because those people have to talk to us. What we do has bite. We can make specific recommendations designed to improve our field unit's performance and its relations with its counterparts—immediate improvements.

The question for companies in trying to accomplish the same thing looms large: Since you can't coerce people in your company to talk with you, how can you incentivize them to do so? The short answer is that you can do what Jack Welch tried to do in his Work-Out program, referenced in Chapter 11: Not only do you make it clear that input can be given directly to a boss, but also that the information, idea, or opinion will be met with respect, not judgment. I explore this further in the discussion later on how to elicit disclosure.

In the Agency, when our inspective audit, or management audit, is completed, it goes to the director and the unit. The unit then gets a chance to reply with retaliations such as "This isn't broken because . . ." or "This can't be fixed because . . ." or "Thanks a lot; we're on it." The upshot is that some IG recommendations are accepted by the director and others are not. For those that are accepted, the unit in question is directed to make the called-for changes within a certain time.

I'm not suggesting that you implement something as regimented as an IG inspection at your organization, but when something goes wrong, the process of discovering lessons learned and then acting on them has to involve two things:

1. Disclosure

2. Change

I addressed the topic of normalizing change—and in this case, it would be planned change—in Chapter 11, so you may want to refer to it after the following discussion of disclosure.

ELICITING DISCLOSURE

Whether you are a case officer or a corporate executive, it's human nature to put a caveat on the concept of full disclosure: Tell 'em everything, but be sure to cover your butt. One reason someone at the National Clandestine

Service might be more inclined to embrace the notion of unqualified full disclosure is the role that discretion plays in daily transactions with colleagues. It's like a club or society that requires its members to keep certain things secret among themselves. You might feel assured sharing sensitive personal facts with a fellow member because he's already demonstrated that he has practice exercising judgment in handling information.

This is a trait of grown-ups, not just spies, but companies generally don't seem to value cultivating it. In fact, I've observed that it's often the opposite behavior that businesspeople are encouraged to adopt. Feel free to say what's on your mind. Spill your guts. Come clean. The result of reinforcing those hackneyed ideas instead of getting complete and coherent information is that you're more likely to hear more words but only a fragmented story. "Full disclosure" and "too much information" are not the same.

Before I illustrate the distinction, consider how and why you might incorporate ongoing policies, formal or informal, that reward people for making mistakes. Good decision making does not necessarily lead to good outcomes, any more than bad decision making necessarily leads to bad outcomes. Sometimes people wearing seatbelts die in car crashes that they might have survived if they weren't wearing the seatbelt. It's rare, but it happens, yet wearing the seatbelt never was a bad decision. Sometimes people make weird or illogical decisions, and they end up making millions in ice cream or automobiles. That's good fortune. It doesn't make the decision a good one; it makes it a lucky one.

Keep this in mind as you invite information and initiative from people on your staff. Pull back from being judgmental. Within the bounds of reason, reward people who try to think creatively and fail, as well as those who think creatively and succeed. They are doing what you want them to do: innovate with the mission in mind. If you welcome their efforts and information consistently, you will find people much more willing to divulge their innermost thoughts when something bad results.

Here is an example of full disclosure in response to the question, "From your perspective, can you give us a clue about the hole in our computer security that just cost us a million dollars?" Answer: "I have very little contact with the IT folks except when I have a problem with my computer. That may point to the problem, in fact. None of us in this division has contact with them until something goes wrong. They may not feel like part of the team, and so they don't care as much about the operation. I admit that I show them about as much regard and attention as people who wash our windows."

The answer signals a specific problem and a route to mitigating it.

Here is an example of fragmented disclosure in response to the same question:

Answer: "The techies are in their own world, and I don't see any evidence that they care about what the rest of us are doing or what the company needs to make money. I'll have them in here to fix something and they get a call on the cell phone and run off because they're so darned important and when they do get back to me, they don't necessarily fix the problem—they do some kind of Band-Aid action. It wouldn't even surprise me if they knew about the security problem and thought it would be good for job security to let it go so they would seem valuable when a problem occurred. The people in PR aren't any better. I heard one of them blabbing all kinds of things to a reporter because the more coverage she gets, the more likely it is that she'll hang on to her job."

The second answer is a rambling, speculative, accusatory response that suggests the solution to the problem is to fire everyone on the IT staff—and maybe the PR manager, too.

To get the kind of answer that's useful and complete, you first have to establish that discretion is valued in your organization and that information itself is considered an asset. Lay down the following two guidelines for both written and oral communication:

1. *Listen; pay attention to the question.* A common problem, and one that's frustrating to effective communicators, is that some people project dimensions and meanings onto a question that aren't intended to be there. Just because you were asked about a computer security breach doesn't mean anyone wants your input on what a PR manager said to a reporter.

2. *Focus on the subject.* You may be a psychologist, but chances are you're not. Your insights as to whether someone is in his own world or has a deep-seated inclination to sabotage the organization don't have credibility until you present facts that point others toward the same conclusion.

LEARNING LESSONS THAT LEAD TO ORGANIZATIONAL IMPROVEMENTS

* Make the process of damage assessment a discrete project unless you have a large enough staff to make someone have an Inspector General's function full time.

* Provide guidance on how you want information communicated. Rambling e-mails or conversation may yield valuable information, but it will take unnecessary extra work to get it.

* On an ongoing basis, pull back from being judgmental when people offer input and ideas for improvement. As appropriate, reward people who try to help and fail as well as those who try to help and succeed.

. . . .

When Advice from a Spy Means Good Business

What faces do you see when you consider who wants, or perhaps needs, the products or services you offer? I don't mean demographic or other descriptive information. I mean real people. The insights in this book on how to build your organization with top performers, collect and vet information so that it becomes intelligence, and overpower your competition will resonate for you when you see those faces.

In my career with the CIA, I belonged to an organization that helped meet Americans' desire for national security by providing the president of the United States with the intelligence he needed and wanted to make decisions. I urge you to be that clear and succinct in describing your work and your customers because then you have a commanding vision of why you should take action to improve your company.

I believe that, in order to do that, you have to make the connection between what you do and how that affects human beings. Maintaining a focus on your customers' needs when they are face to face is easy. Doing it when your customers are not watching, waiting, or asking for something presents a different challenge.

Like most people working for a huge company, case officers rarely have contact with our main customer—the president of the United States. We do have the advantage of knowing what he looks like, though. Having a picture in your head of your customers provides enormous advantages in fulfilling the day-to-day requirements of your job, as well as having big ideas about how to take your organization to a new level.

Here at the International Spy Museum, all I have to do is go downstairs and walk around the museum floor to see the reason we come to work every day. It's the teenagers discovering cryptography, adults roleplaying as though they were characters in a John Le Carré novel, and groups of kids from a local elementary school who sit in entranced silence as they watch a movie on the role of intelligence in national security.

If you work for a trade association of pharmaceutical companies, the faces of your customers are the people sitting next to you in committee meetings or wandering through the halls on their way to meet your boss. If you work for a pharmaceutical company, it's not your customers (i.e., physicians) who keep you going as much as it is their customers—asthma sufferers, people battling cancer, elderly folks trying to avoid getting the flu.

Getting this visual connection is a lot harder when you make cars, dig for oil, or write software. It's true that you may enjoy the work itself, or have the practical satisfaction of getting paid a lot, but people somewhere benefit from what you do every day. Do what you can to keep those people in mind, and you will strengthen your motivation to implement the suggestions given in this book.

GLOSSARY

• • • • • • • • • • • • • • • • •

Agent—A person who volunteers or who is recruited by a case officer to provide information or other services covertly to the CIA.

Asset—Possibly an agent, but perhaps someone or something else that facilitates clandestine operations; could refer to a clandestine capability, such as phone taps, safe houses, surveillance vehicles, and the like, available to a CIA field facility.

Baseline—The way a person speaks and behaves under normal, or relatively stimulus-free, conditions.

Case officer—A person employed by the Central Intelligence Agency's National Clandestine Service (see below) who is responsible for recruiting and running agents and other clandestine activity, including covert action.

CIA—Central Intelligence Agency.

Cold War—The political, ideological, and near-military conflict between the United States and the former Soviet Union between (effectively) 1947 and 1991.

Covert action—Intelligence operations directed at clandestinely influencing events abroad, including propaganda, political intervention, and paramilitary operations.

DCI—Director of Central Intelligence, the person with authority over the CIA and the Intelligence Community; with the establishment of a Director of National Intelligence (DNI) on the recommendation of the 9/11 Commission, the DNI oversees the Intelligence Community and the DCIA oversees the CIA alone.

Dead drop—A place where materials can be concealed for later retrieval by a clandestine contact, such as a case officer or agent; could refer to the manner of leaving sensitive materials, for example, in a hollow rock.

Denied area—A term used by the CIA to designate those countries considered aggressively hostile to clandestine operations by the CIA.

DO—Directorate of Operations, one of four directorates in the CIA; now the National Clandestine Service.

Elicitation techniques—Codified practices relying on psychology, not physical contact, to get people to talk about sensitive subjects.

Engaged employee—Someone mentally energized and committed to realizing the mission and living the values of the organization.

Exfiltration operation—Using clandestine procedures to smuggle an agent, and perhaps his family, out of his home country.

Failure of imagination—Term coined by historian Roberta Wohlstetter (1962) to describe a reason the United States did not consider that Japan might attack Pearl Harbor.

Farm, the—An unofficial designation of a major CIA training facility.

HUMINT—An abbreviation for human intelligence, describing recruitment operations to collect intelligence from human sources.

IMINT—An abbreviation for image intelligence.

Inspector General (IG)—A presidentially appointed CIA official charged with internal oversight; the IG appointment is subject to U.S. Senate approval.

Intelligence—Refers to the process and the product of collecting, analyzing, and disseminating information from a wide range of secret and open sources on matters bearing on national security.

Intelligence estimates—Extrapolations based on best available information.

International Spy Museum—The first and only public museum in the world solely dedicated to the people and craft of espionage.

KGB—The acronym for the lead Soviet organization for security, police, and intelligence; the equivalent to the CIA during the Cold War; during the Cold War, this massive Soviet organization incorporated the wide range of responsibilities exercised by the CIA and the FBI in the United States. The KGB's military counterpart was the GRU, which also carried out clandestine operations.

Magnetic culture—A term trademarked by Human Solutions and coined by founder Kevin Sheridan to describe an environment that draws top talent into an organization and continuously attracts that talent, making it very difficult for high performers to leave.

MICE—An acronym for some major factors leading individuals to commit espionage: money, ideology, coercion, and ego.

Mirror-imaging—Seeing yourself in another—it could be a person, an organization, or a country—to the extent that you do not see what is really there; a variation of a failure of imagination; considered one of the worst analytical hazards.

Moscow Rules—An unofficial working list of brief guidelines for case officers handling CIA agents in Moscow in the face of constant KGB surveillance; former CIA officer Tony Mendez describes the list in his informative book, *The Master of Disguise.*

National Clandestine Service (NCS)—The clandestine arm of the Central Intelligence Agency (CIA) and the national authority for the coordination, de-confliction, and evaluation of clandestine operations across the Intelligence Community of the United States (official CIA definition).

OSINT—An abbreviation for open-source intelligence, meaning any form of printed or electronic media available to the public, such as newspapers, magazines, TV, the Internet, and so on.

OSS—Office of Strategic Services, the World War II U.S. foreign intelligence collection and covert action organization disbanded at the end of the war, considered the predecessor to the Central Intelligence Agency.

Outcome thinking—A predictive exercise to determine how to sequence actions in order to get the best outcome, not necessarily the predetermined one.

Perseveration—A British intelligence service term for flawed intelligence analysis when analysts get stuck in what they conclude early on and then find data to support that theory.

PHOTINT—An abbreviation for photographic intelligence, which refers to the way the information is collected.

Precedence indicator—Alerts on communications from the field that tell the recipient how time-sensitive and important the information is; normal traffic would have no indicator, whereas something with a measure of urgency would be marked "priority"; something more pressing, "immediate." The extreme is "flash," requiring instant attention.

Proximate reality—Coming as close to the facts as possible, given that you are dealing with imperfect information.

Reading in—Exposing yourself to every scrap of information you can find about a new location and situation and the people there before encountering them.

Safe house—Typically a private residence with no official tie-in that could be used for agent meetings; a site that case officers would consider safe to house or meet with someone of interest.

SIGINT—An abbreviation for signals intelligence, referring to clandestine intercepts of electronic or other communications.

SIS—Senior Intelligence Service; the Intelligence Community equivalent of the Executive Branch's Senior Executive Service (SES), which equates roughly to flag rank in the U.S. military, for example, an SIS-1 would equate to a one-star general.

Socratic method—One way to approach analysis that involves learning through questions and answers, with the underlying assumption that the people engaged in the exchange have some differences of opinion.

Spy—From the perspective of an Agency case officer, someone from another government engaging in espionage, although loosely applied, it refers to any of us in the espionage business.

Spycraft—Methods that spies use to conduct operations (also see Tradecraft).

Tradecraft—Methods that case officers and others in the National Clandestine Service use to conduct their operations.

USSR—Union of Soviet Socialist Republics, which formally dissolved in 1991.

SOURCE MATERIAL AND RECOMMENDED READING

Allen, Thomas B. 2008. *Declassified: 50 Top Secret Documents That Changed History.* Washington, D.C.: National Geographic.

Allen, Thomas B., and Norman Polmar. 2004. *Spy Book: The Encyclopedia of Espionage,* 2nd ed. New York: Random House.

Armstrong, Willis C., William Leonhart, William J. McCaffrey, and Herbert C. Rothenbert. 1984. "The Hazards of Single-Outcome Forecasting." *Studies in Intelligence,* 28, no. 3: 57–70.

Barth, Jack. 2004. *The Handbook of Practical Spying.* Washington, D.C.: National Geographic. Introduction by Peter Earnest.

Bull, George. "The Elicitation Interview." *Studies in Intelligence,* 14, no. 2 (Fall 1970): 115–122.

Clarridge, Duane. 1977. *A Spy for All Seasons.* New York: Scribner.

Czajkowski, Anthony F. 1959. "Techniques of Domestic Intelligence Collection." *Studies in Intelligence,* 3, no. 1 (Winter): 69–83. [Originally classified CONFIDENTIAL.]

Deveny, Kathleen. 2009. "Reinventing Newsweek." *Newsweek,* May 11.

Devlin, Larry. 2007. *Chief of Station, Congo: Fighting the Cold War in a Hot Zone.* New York: Public Affairs.

Dickey, Christopher. 2010. *Securing the City: Inside America's Best Counterterror Force—NYPD.* New York: Simon & Schuster.

Dickey, Christopher. 2009. "The Spymaster of New York." *Newsweek,* February 9.

Dobson, Michael, and Deborah Singer Dobson. 1999. *Managing Up!* New York: AMACOM.

Dujmovic, Nicholas. 2008. "Commemorating the Dead at CIA." *Studies in Intelligence,* 52, no. 3: 3–16.

Gallup. 2008. "Honesty and Ethics."

Gregg, Donald P. 2009. "Speaking with the Enemy." *International Herald Tribune,* February 9.

Haines, Gerald K., and Robert E. Leggett. 2001. *CIA's Analysis of the Soviet Union 1947–1991.* Washington, D.C.: Central Intelligence Agency.

Hartley, Gregory, and Maryann Karinch. 2010. *The Body Language Handbook: How to Read Everyone's Hidden Intentions.* Franklin Lakes, N.J.: Career Press.

————. 2007. *I Can Read You Like a Book.* Franklin Lakes, N.J.: Career Press.

Helms, Richard. 2003. *A Look over My Shoulder.* New York: Random House.

Hohl, Dean, and Maryann Karinch. 2003. *Rangers Lead the Way: The Army Rangers' Guide to Leading Your Organization Through Chaos.* Avon, Mass.: Adams Media.

Kent, Sherman. "The Need for an Intelligence Literature." *Studies in Intelligence,* 1, no. 1 (September 1955): 1–8.

Kessler, Ronald. 1992. *Inside the CIA: Revealing the Secrets of the World's Most Powerful Spy Agency.* New York: Pocket Books.

Lathrop, Charles E., Ed. 2004. *The Literary Spy.* New Haven, Conn.: Yale University Press.

Lawson, Willow. 2005. "Good Boss, Bad Boss." *Psychology Today,* November 1.

McCormick, James. 2008. *The Power of Risk.* San Francisco: Maxwell Press.

McKee, W.J. "The Reports Office: Issues of Quality." *Studies in Intelligence,* 27, no. 1 (Spring 1983): 11–18.

Melton, H. Keith. 1996. *The Ultimate Spy Book.* New York: DK Publishing. Forewords by William Colby and Oleg Kalugin.

Mendez, Antonio J. 1999. *The Master of Disguise: My Secret Life in the CIA.* New York: William Morrow.

Mendez, Antonio, and Jonna Mendez. 2002. *SpyDust: Two Masters of Disguise Reveal the Tools and Operations That Helped Win the Cold War*. New York: Atria.

Neimark, Ira. 2007. *Crossing Fifth Avenue to Bergdorf Goodman*. New York: Specialist Press International.

Parloff, Roger. 2009. "More Brazen Than Madoff?" *Fortune* (April 1, 2009): 59–66.

Pink, Daniel H. 2006. *A Whole New Mind: Why Right-Brainers Will Rule the Future*. New York: Riverhead Trade.

Post, Jerrold M. 1975. "The Anatomy of Treason." *Studies in Intelligence*, 19, no. 2: 36–37.

Quirk, John. 1988. *CIA Entrance Examination*. New York: Simon & Schuster. Foreword by William E. Colby.

Rasmussen Reports. 2007. "22% Believe Bush Knew About 9/11 Attacks in Advance." May 4.

Ries, Al, and Jack Trout. 1994. *22 Immutable Laws of Marketing*. New York: HarperBusiness.

Sherman, Kent. 1955. "The Need for an Intelligence Literature." *Studies in Intelligence*, 1, no. 1: 1–8.

Wallace, Robert, and H. Keith Melton. 2008. *Spycraft: The Secret History of the CIA's Spytechs from Communism to Al-Qaeda*. New York: Penguin Group.

Weber, Ralph E. 2002. *Spymasters: Ten CIA Officers in Their Own Words*. Wilmington, Del.: SR Books.

Weiser, Benjamin. 2004. *A Secret Life: The Polish Officer, His Covert Mission, and the Price He Paid to Save His Country*. New York: Public Affairs.

Westerfield, H. Bradford, Ed. 1995. *Inside the CIA's Private World: Declassified Articles from the Agency's Internal Journal 1955–1992*. New Haven, Conn.: Yale University Press.

Wohlstetter, Roberta. 1962. *Pearl Harbor: Warning and Decision*. Palo Alto, Calif.: Stanford University Press.

INDEX